What Others Are Saying

"A pleasant, compassionate, creative, and mindful guide to personal finance. This book makes you feel better about the process as you learn. You really feel like the author is holding your hand and lightening the load along the way." -KM

"Honestly, this is the best self-help book I've read in a while. I loved the different approach to money management. The book opens up your mindset to make your money work for you, instead of just tirelessly working for your money. I appreciated the practical advice." -MT

"One of the most thoughtful guides to money and mental wellness that I have read. A work of art in style and content." -MK

"The human aspect, the permission to feel, the feeling that the author treated me like a valued friend, neither patronizing nor silly, made this book incredibly unique and valuable." -DG

"An encouraging, informative, friendly book about finance, which is so rare for this topic." -LF

"The book has excellent questions that made me stop and think about goals, support systems, and opening my mind to other ideas – not just money." -DT

"I particularly liked comparing a relationship with money to a relationship with a friend or family member. The encouraging, flexible approach to different methods of money management felt refreshing and safe." -BC

"The author doesn't just tell you to "make a budget" or "have a balance sheet." Instead, she shows you practical methods and attitudes to make these things happen. It makes it emotionally possible to do things that are intimidating." -FJ

Peaceful Prosperity

Taking the Fear Out of Finance

Laura Redfern, CFP®, CeFT®

Lotus Tribe Studios, LLC

Lotus Tribe Studios

1001 S. Capital of Texas Hwy, Ste M-100

Austin, TX 78746

Publisher's Note: while based on true events, the characters and events in this book have been fictionalized. Some names and characteristics have been changed, some events have been compressed, and some dialogue has been recreated.

Disclaimer: Please note that the author makes no guarantees about the results of the information applied from this material. Educational and informational resources are shared with the intent to help you succeed in improving your relationship with finances. You nevertheless need to know that your ultimate success or failure will be the result of your own efforts, your particular situation, and innumerable other circumstances beyond the author's knowledge or control.

Edited by Anna Jaworski / Baby Hearts Press and Amy M. Le / Quill Hawk Publishing

Cover Design by Omer Farooq

ISBN (paperback) 978-1-960932-03-7

ISBN (ebook) 978-1-960932-02-0

Dedication

To my mom, for being my original inspiration, editor, friend,
and biggest fan.

What larks!

Contents

Acknowledgements and Thanks

To Tina, for her vision that started us off; to Jean, for her encouragement and tenacity; to Dennis, for his coaching and insight.

To Lisa, for being a role model; to Allison, for her enthusiasm; to Amy, for her positivity and support.

To Anna, for her mentorship, friendship, and for believing in me.

To every client I have had the honor to work with – you have inspired and taught me more than you will probably ever know.

To Ryan, for his assistance, faith, and unending patience.

To Susan, Jesse, Michael, Roger, Carrie, Polly, Jean, Joan, and all my FTI family, who helped me to step outside my comfort zone, embrace the mess, and grow wiser as a result.

To Lisa, Bari, Barbara, Dr. Jo, and Draye, for their wonderful words, ideas, and collaboration.

To Amy, Frank, Joanna, Josh, and my new writing family, who welcomed me into a whole new world with open arms.

To Jessica, Kyle, Catherine, Juan, Stephen, Valerie, R1, T2, Kris, Charlie, Mary Pat, Pam, Kerri, Mark, Anna, Frank, and all my Toastmasters family, for providing wonderful and honest feedback that helped me to think outside the box.

To Missy, Monica, Sara, Brittany, and all the women who attended the "Peaceful Prosperity" and/or "Financial Freedom for Females" Workshops - you have helped me create this for all women.

To my beta readers, for sharing their valuable time and invaluable insights with me, to make this book the best it can be.

And finally, to the birds in my backyard who came to visit my feeder while I was writing - thanks for reminding me to fly.

Foreword by Susan K Bradley, CFP®, CeFT®

Founder of Sudden Money Institute and Financial Transitionist Institute

The title of this book, *Peaceful Prosperity*, is exactly what you can experience with the guidance Laura Redfern offers both in her book and the companion workbook.

I have read more than my share of self-help finance books. Many provide excellent information. Some provide well-structured workbooks. So far none have come close to the depth and warmth of this book. I know that is a big claim. It is also my honest assessment and my personal experience.

Every one of us human beings has a personal relationship with money. We all have beliefs about money that influence the quality of that relationship. Peaceful is not a word most people would use to describe their finances. We need to have our attention on how we use money in our life to support our relationships, values, beliefs, dreams, and responsibilities. This takes more than a good credit rating, a retirement savings account, or spending carefully.

In this book, Laura will invite you to step back from your numbers and experience the 'why' behind your choices, beliefs, and for many of us, our fears about this pervasive topic. As you move through the chapters and the workbook, you may find new clarity that leads you to new insights and possibilities. The surprise awaiting you is the discovery that many of the obstacles to peace and prosperity in your life are your own creation. This book will empower you to create new systems for building the life you want.

It is true that some people do feel both peace and prosperity. For some, it just comes naturally most of the time. The rest of us can achieve that lovely balance with a combination of intention, attention, and shifts in our internal dialogue and beliefs. All of us, regardless of the balance we have achieved and the amount of money we have, need to have the ability to absorb the life changes that are part of our human experience.

What Laura offers readers of this book is a way to build a foundation of well-being that can absorb the disruption or the upset of life-altering events and the transitions that follow.

I personally know Laura through her work with me at the Financial Transitionist Institute. Over the years I have known her, she has always shown up as someone committed to advancing her skills to better serve her clients at all stages of their lives. Many aspire to the level of dedication and service she provides; only a small percentage have the staying power to keep going.

This book reflects who Laura is as a person and as a financial planner, especially her belief that anyone can create a life of peace and prosperity. She told me she wrote the book as a love letter to her mother. I see it as a love letter to anyone who reads it.

Preface

I want to talk with you about money.

We all have a love-hate relationship with money, don't we?

It's something that we may feel controls us – like a bossy acquaintance, dictating what we can or cannot do, sticking its unwanted nose into our business, judging every nook and cranny of our lives. We may harbor resentment, anger, or fear toward money. We may feel embarrassed or ashamed that we don't know more about how money works. We may feel small next to people we see relating to money with apparent ease, confidence, or knowledge. We may say things like, "I'm not good with money" or "I just don't understand money" or WORSE – we may not talk about money AT ALL.

Talking about money isn't easy. But it's really, truly, deeply important. Not because you need to be rich or buy everything you want. I say money is really, truly, deeply important because it goes way deeper than the surface. It touches upon our sense of self-worth, our confidence (or lack thereof), our relationships, and our identities. WHO WE ARE and how we operate in the world are influenced by our relationship with money. Our relationship with money influences how we operate in the world and WHO WE ARE. The good news is when one of those aspects improves, so does the other.

As a friend and meditation teacher likes to say, "How you do anything is how you do everything." The way you relate to money affects the way you relate to your family, your coworkers, your friends, and your community.

In 2010, my father's company closed up shop, forcing my father into early retirement. Finances were tight, to say the least. My mother and father never complained, though (at least not that I know of). They just made it work. They buckled down, cut expenses, got creative at times, and did what they had to do. I found this remarkable, admirable, and inspiring.

When I mentioned this to my mother one day, she seemed surprised. "Really?" she asked. "Honestly I have been feeling ashamed that we have so little money." She had felt embarrassed by her creative solutions to make ends meet. Internally, she had told herself: "I'm not doing a good job. If I were, we'd have more money." (Ironically, this was the same thing my father had told himself, but they never revealed this to each other.) Apparently, I turned this negative self-talk on its head by admiring their budgeting skills. My mother was speechless.

Looking back at that moment several years later, my mother said, "That was a turning point for me." That moment of recognition, of realization, of new perspective, changed her life and her relationship with money forever. It wasn't about "unlocking the key to wealth" or "cracking the code of the stock market." It was about recognizing she had strengths. It was about seeing her world differently. It was about believing in possibilities (like, "maybe I am a decent money manager!"). It was about feeling a new sense of confidence like she never had before.

Peaceful Prosperity is all about that feeling. Sure, it's often experienced by learning cool stuff (which we will do), but the feeling is the key.

Anyone who tells you that finance and feelings have no place together is missing an essential part of the puzzle. Trying to piece together your money puzzle without including the emotional pieces results in a very unsatisfying puzzle full of holes. It doesn't look right, it doesn't feel right, and it doesn't help us find the things we seek: happiness, comfort, security, freedom, abundance, ease.

The way to experience these great things is through an honest exploration of our assumptions. How do we believe money operates in our lives and in the world? Exploring this bravely allows us to choose what we do next. We get to dwell in possibility, rather than stay stuck in old beliefs and habits that we may learned and accepted before we were even aware of what was going on.

I dwell in Possibility –

A fairer House than Prose –

More numerous of Windows –

Superior – for Doors –

—Emily Dickinson

Let me tell you, dwelling in possibility is so much more pleasant than living in a world where you feel stupid, helpless, or trapped. You don't have to live in that world. Possibility is a state of mind. But it is also a learned skill, and you can learn it. You're here, aren't you? That is what we are going to do. First, to show you the possibilities in the world of PEACEFUL PROSPERITY. Then, to help you live it.

Introduction

The Personal Side of Money

I often find that when people come to me for financial advice, they get more than they bargained for. A conversation about the stock market? Sure. Tips on how to save for a future goal? You bet. Observations about the financial opportunities currently available? Absolutely.

But there's so much more.

What about the potential impact that your financial decisions may have on those you love? Or your values and how these show up in your financial behavior? Or your sense of identity, who you are, and what you want to do in this world? In other words, why are you even bothering with all this financial stuff in the first place? Often people don't expect that kind of conversation with a financial advisor.

Simon Sinek, well known for his motivational books and inspirational TED Talk "Start with Why," has said:

Achievement happens when we pursue and attain what we want. Success comes when we are in clear pursuit of why we want it.

If my job is to help people improve their financial lives, we must address not only the technical nuts and bolts of those lives, but also the drivers behind them. The "why," not just the "how" and the "what."

Interestingly, there didn't used to be much formal training for this way of looking at finances. Back in 2011, when I earned my CERTIFIED FINANCIAL PLANNER™ designation, we were well-trained in the nuts-and-bolts areas: estate planning, taxation, employee benefits, insurance, retirement savings, investments, etc. But the "human" side was simply not addressed. Personal financial drivers like relationships, emotions, hopes, dreams, and self-esteem were not considered particularly relevant. Finance is supposed to take the emotion out of money, right?

Wrong.

I am happy to say that the profession is changing. Now, there are designations such as Behavioral Financial Advisor (which my colleague Phil holds), Certified Financial Transitionist (which I hold), Certified Financial Wellness Educator, Registered Life Planner, and even Financial Therapist. These certifications are a wonderful recognition in the financial services profession that human beings are not simply computers. It's nice that someone finally woke up and realized, "Hey, guys! We might serve people better when we acknowledge the human being in front of us instead of focusing only on the numbers."

So that's where we start. With you, the human.

How to Use this Book

T his book is best read in order. Think of it as a journey up your financial mountain. Part One establishes your foundation, your "base camp," if you will. Part Two builds upon that foundation, helping you to strengthen your muscles and practice useful habits as you begin your climb. Part Three helps you to expand and open up your financial world to greater possibilities as you gaze out from your summit and create your vision.

Like any journey, it's best to take it one step at a time, but the pace is up to you. Just remember to keep breathing – and keep climbing.

The companion *Peaceful Prosperity Workbook* is a helpful tool for you to put the ideas in this book to work. It is not essential to buy the *Workbook* to enjoy this book, but you may find the journey more meaningful and the ideas more pertinent to you by using the *Workbook* and engaging in the activities. Overall, the entire series was created to help you discover and create Peaceful Prosperity in your life. Enjoy!

BASE CAMP: PREPARING YOUR FOUNDATION

"The journey of a thousand miles begins with a single step."

-Lao Tzu

Chapter One: Money Mindset

Chapter One

Money Mindset

You're braver than you believe, stronger than you seem, and smarter than you think.

— *Winnie the Pooh*

P eople often come in to my office with little confidence in their knowledge, skills, or power when it comes to finance. I love to remind them what Winne the Pooh said, because it's true. Especially for women, it seems. Every woman I've ever talked to or worked with has had better financial instincts than she gave herself credit for. Seriously. You can do this, ladies! Better yet – you already have. You may just not recognize it. Yet.

But I know that you have all the tools—the instincts if not yet all the skills—to obtain what you desire. Women are naturally wired to be VERY GOOD at this. (Don't believe me? Check out Fidelity Investment's 2021 "Women and Investing Study" – it's just one of many such research findings.) We get intimidated and thrown off by the walls that generations have put up before us that convince us we are dumb, that it's too hard, that we can't...

Don't believe them.

You are brave, strong, smart – and worthy.

Our job in this book is to uncover the tools you already possess. I believe you lack nothing. You may not be able to see it just yet, but I can see it. I have been up financial mountains many times, and I have led many women, just like you. I know the beautiful vistas up there as well as the potential pitfalls. And together we can climb this.

Uncovering the Money Myths

When were any of us taught this money stuff? It was "never" for me. How about you?

So why do we beat ourselves up for not knowing how to manage money? Or for not feeling "natural" or comfortable with money topics?

Picture a young child who is learning to play the piano. Would you expect this child to sit down and bust out a Mozart concerto on their first try? I doubt it. More likely, you would applaud them as they plunked away, even if it wasn't particularly melodious at first. You would encourage them to keep practicing scales and arpeggios. You'd be impressed when they mastered "Mary Had a Little Lamb." Mozart may come, but you wouldn't expect it on the first day, month, or year.

So why don't we take that same level of encouragement, patience, and grace that we'd give to a learning child and show that to ourselves when learning a new skill like finance? Why do we tend to be so unforgiving and hard on ourselves? I believe it is largely because of the money stories we carry with us.

My mom raised me to be fiercely independent. She told me ever since I was a tiny child that I didn't need a man; I could stand on my own two feet. I could do anything. "YOU GO, GIRL!" was tattooed on my forehead from a young age.

And I believed it – for myself. But I began to observe that my mom didn't believe it for herself. My mom was a strong woman. She was a smart woman. Growing up, I observed that she knew what she was doing. And YET... every time she took out the checkbook and went to her desk, she told a different story—with her body language. Her shoulders hunched, her brow furrowed, and her mood soured. We kids knew NOT to go near mom when she took out her checkbook. Where was the disconnect? Why would a woman who was strong in every other aspect of her life show fear when it came to finance? What was going on here? I was curious.

We weren't super poor or super rich, by the way. We were comfortable. My mom was a great money manager. A stay-at-home parent, she would allocate the money that my dad brought in and make it all work out. We had food on the table, we had school clothes every fall, and we had holiday parties and birthday parties. Life was great. But my mom didn't feel that way. And it all seemed to do with money. She wasn't comfortable with money. She always thought she was doing something wrong. She wasn't, but the voices in her head – the money story that she was carrying – told her otherwise.

In the movie Lord of the Rings (yes, I am one of THOSE people... a fantasy fan... but stay with me!) there is a memorable scene on a mountain. The heroes of the story are trying to cross a mountain (in the movie it is called Caradhras) and they are having a heck of a time. The temperatures are freezing, causing icicles to form on their clothes. Snow is swirling in the air, making it nearly impossible to see. Rocks fall from the top of the mountain, nearly crushing them to pieces. The mountain seems insurmountable.

But one of the characters notices something: all this chaos is not coming from the mountain. "A foul voice is on the air," he says. It is the evil wizard Saruman who is casting dark spells from his castle far away. It is he who is causing all this chaos and confusion. It is not the mountain. The mountain, is, in fact, neutral. The mountain is not the enemy. The evil wizard is.

Each of us has an evil wizard in our heads, who conjures up clouds of shame, doubt, uncertainty, and fear, making it difficult to see our financial situation clearly.

This wizard may come from our upbringing, our cultural background, or our schooling. It could be something we were taught long ago, something we experienced, or something we observed – or none of the above. Wherever he comes from, this wizard takes away our true power. He makes us feel it is impossible to climb the mountain.

Don't listen to this foul voice on the air. This voice is not telling you the truth.

Our first tool on this journey will help you get to the root of your "foul voices" and discover where these voices are coming from. It is a wonderful worksheet from Barbara Stanny called "Digging Down to the Roots." It lists 12 questions to consider. I include them here but I encourage you to write them down somewhere or use the *Peaceful Prosperity Workbook* which contains the questions and space to write about your reflections.

"Digging Down to the Roots" From Overcoming Underearning by Barbara Stanny

Complete the following sentences with the first words that come to mind. Don't censure what you get or look for the "right" answer. Let yourself go with your very first reaction. And do it quickly. You can always change your responses later.

1. My biggest fear about money is...

2. My father felt money was...

3. My mother felt money was...

4. In my family, money caused...

5. My early experience with money was...

6. Money equals...

7. I'm afraid if I had more money, I would...

8. In order to have more money, I'd need to...

9. When I have money, I usually...

10. If I could afford it, I would...

11. People with money are...

12. I'd have more money if...

As you dig deep into these questions, be gentle with yourself. You may have never thought about this before. Or maybe you have, at some point. Either way, recognize that every one of us has an evil voice in our heads that can conjure up fear and chaos. It is important to realize that this voice is not your authentic voice. It has been conjured up over the years of your life. It is probably so familiar that you may have convinced yourself that it is the voice of "reality" or "sensibility" when in fact, it is not.

It could be that the negative, nay-saying voice is not even yours. Think about it. Is that part of someone else's baggage? Are you carrying your brother's suitcase full of rocks up your financial mountain? Or your mom's? Or someone else's?

You may feel you have to lug that suitcase all the way up to the summit, but you don't. It's not yours to carry. It's not your job. Your job is to let this rock suitcase GO.

Letting go is essential before you climb. That's why we start with this exercise! If you don't let go of this baggage, the climb is going to be harder. When you do let go of it, you will be amazed by what you can accomplish.

In the workshops, we work through this discovery process together. I have been honored to have witnessed this transformation of letting go and the profound effect it can have.

For example: Maureen had an epiphany when she pondered question #7: "I'm afraid if I had more money, I would..." For her, it was "be like Aunt Kiki."

"Nobody wanted to be like Aunt Kiki," she shared. "She was a miserable old biddy who was disliked by everyone in the family. We all knew she had plenty of money, but she would never spend it on anything or anyone. One memorable Christmas, she gave every family member a box of tissues as a gift. And they weren't even the good tissues – they were a cheap off-brand!" She laughed. "The family has talked about that insult for years. So I think that kind of was embedded in my mind, that if you were rich and had a lot of money, you would end up like her – someone who was old and bitter and unhappy and alone. Someone the rest of the family hated." She stopped with a look of surprise on her face.

"Do you know other people who have money and aren't like that?" I asked.

"Well, sure..." she continued. "I had another aunt and uncle who were incredibly kind. But I didn't see them much because they lived far away. And I don't think I knew they were wealthy until much later. I just remember when they visited, they had nice clothes and would take us to cool museums and stuff. I remember once my uncle bought me the BEST chocolate sundae EVER..." She laughed, lost in the memory. "I never really made that connection before – that rich people could be like that, instead of like Aunt Kiki."

In psychology, this is called "cognitive dissonance." Something you believe is met by some evidence to the contrary that you can't refute, and your brain goes "boing" like a spring that comes loose. You simply can't hold on to the old belief anymore.

The cognitive dissonance Maureen experienced at that moment shocked her brain out of the old belief and freed her to think and act differently.

I saw her two years later and she told me since that realization, she had been amazed by how much easier it had been for her to save money. She had paid off her credit cards. She made the final payment on her mortgage. Now she was focused on retirement – which I am convinced will be a much happier experience now that she has kicked the Aunt Kiki mindset.

Kicking an old mindset isn't easy. As the saying goes, "old habits die hard." Some of these money beliefs you may have always accepted as true without ever looking at them. Now you have the opportunity to take a good look at those old beliefs and reconsider.

This happened to Janice, another workshop participant. She shared her story about her answer to question #11: "People with money are..."

"When I was growing up, for years, I used to think people with money were evil and must have done awful things to get rich. I mean, there's no other way to get rich, right?" There was a twinkle in her eye that suggested she was being ironic. "That was my narrative and I never questioned it."

Janice continued, "Not until high school. I was in a club with a girl named Allison, who was hands down one of the nicest people I'd ever met. Not sticky-sweet fake nice. Like genuinely kind and helpful to others. She was super bright and helped peers who struggled with their homework. She was generous with her time, her knowledge, and her beautiful smile. And yet she was humble. She played on the soccer team, and whenever the team did well, she always credited her teammates for their skills, never calling attention to hers."

"I'm sure that Allison had her flaws, but that's not the point. What I learned later, that knocked me over, was not about her flaws. It was about her family. I later learned that Allison came from THE wealthiest family in town. What? It didn't make sense to me. I thought, 'But... that isn't what rich people act like. They are evil and snobby jerks or penny-pinching selfish robbers... aren't they?' Well, obviously not! That moment changed my whole opinion about rich people, and I am so grateful. It changed the direction of my life, just in that one realization."

Janice's cognitive dissonance led her to a different way of thinking. She opened up to the idea that being wealthy didn't mean you had to be an evil person. That idea was a revelation; it started her off on a new career path, where she ultimately became very successful and wealthy.

If you were in a workshop with me right now, I would hand you a pair of earmuffs. I would say, "When negative voices come into your head, I want you to take out these earmuffs and put them on. Think of me telling you, 'Don't give these voices your attention.' Instead, strengthen the other voices in your head by giving them your attention."

What other voices? Well, there are other voices inside your head. If you stop for a moment, you can hear them. They can be difficult to hear but your authentic voice—call it your soul, your higher self, your inner wisdom, your fairy godmother—is there somewhere. It can be very soft and quiet, especially if we aren't used to tuning in to what it has to say.

But you can tune in. Doing the "Digging Down to the Roots" activity is a powerful start. Meditation and mindfulness practices can help to get in tune with your authentic voice, as well.

Think of it like a radio dial. Your inner voice is the channel that talks about living the life you were meant to live, becoming the person you want to be, and leaving the legacy you want to leave in the world. It knows you can do this. Turn it up.

You can experiment with turning up the volume on your authentic voice by asking it what it has to say. Invite it to share. You may find, in time, that it is a powerful ally in helping you to overcome the harsher, louder voices you may have been listening to—those "foul voices on the air." Can you change the channel?

Sometimes the "foul voices" show up in unusual ways. For example, Kaitlyn was sad when it came to answering question #8: "In order to have more money, I'd need to..." She said wistfully, "...be a different person." She obviously didn't want to be a different person. So she believed that she would never have more money.

I asked her to explore that a little more. "Why would you need to be a different person to have more money?" I asked.

"Well, like my friends who have a lot of money. I think about them and I think, they sold out to big tech. They work these long hours and are slaves to the big corporation they work for. I don't want to do that, even if it does mean making more money."

"I get that!" I said. "Do you know anyone else with money who isn't like that?"

She thought for a moment, and I watched as an idea dawned on her like the morning sun. "Actually, yes, I do," she said. "I have some other friends in California and they're not like that. They have a very different lifestyle. More relaxed. They're not selling out or anything like that. Their work is meaningful. It helps people. Like, they are actually doing good in the world."

"But they're still making money?" I nudged.

"Yeah." She seemed puzzled by how this could happen. "They are making money." And then came an even more powerful realization. "They're not even employed full-time! I mean, they work, but it's in several jobs. They have a couple of different part-time gigs. It's not a traditional work setup."

"Sounds great," I said. "Is there anything wrong with that?"

"No," she said with wonder. "Wow! Oh my gosh, I have been struggling with my sense of self-worth, thinking I was being irresponsible if I didn't have a full-time adult job. I was feeling like I was never going to get ahead. And here all along I have these friends who are doing this differently... I just wasn't seeing the options."

"Maybe you could hang out with these friends some more. Ask them how they make it work, and see if that is a model for what you can do."

I wish you could have seen the sense of relief and excitement on her face.

Not all money stories are negative. When Jenny considered question #5: "My early experience with money was..." she surprised us all by saying, "It was FUN!"

"I don't often hear that," I observed. "What was fun about it?"

"My earliest experiences with money that I can remember all had to do with our neighborhood garage sale," she said. "My mom and my two aunts would supervise a big garage sale every spring. My mom encouraged me and my younger brother to think about all our toys and sell the ones we didn't play with anymore. I was always very selective, but my brother would sell anything that wasn't nailed down! He usually had some new video game he wanted to buy, so he would wheel and deal with anyone who came by, trying to convince them to buy his toys." We chuckled at this idea.

"And you?" I asked. "Why was it fun for you?"

"My aunt kept a big ledger and I just loved seeing how it all worked... how it was all so organized. When I sold something, she'd mark it in the ledger, and then at the end of the day, she would add it all up. I can remember watching her count all the coins and the bills to make certain everything was reconciled.

Then she'd put our money into envelopes and hand it to us. I felt like an adult! I felt on top of the world!"

When she became an adult, Jenny was able to capture that feeling of being "on top of the world" that she had experienced as a kid. "I think that early experience helped me a lot," she said. "I'm not afraid of money because I can remember that feeling." Do you have positive memories about money? It may be a good time to explore them, too.

Getting to the root of our money stories can impact our relationships in profound ways. This is another wonderful discovery I've seen from the "Roots" exercise.

Carrie discovered this when she pondered question #6, "Money equals..."

"I said power," she confessed. "That comes from watching my parents when I was a kid, and seeing how my dad used money to keep power over my mom."

"Like, he didn't even let her know how much money he actually made. He would give her an allowance, and she had to make the household work on what he gave her. If she wanted to give us girls ballet lessons over the summer, she'd either have to beg him for the extra money or go without something else so she could pay for it."

"I think that's why I've always been nervous about talking about money with my husband. He's great, but in my head, I guess I'm always thinking, 'What is he hiding from me?' And it's been really important to me to know where all the money is and what's going on. I don't want to be a victim like my mom." She was quiet for a moment. "So now I am realizing why I've always had this weird emotional reaction to money—why I always feel the need for control, even though my husband has never, ever done anything to make me not trust him."

I want to emphasize here that the key to this inner exploration is empathy and kindness. Judgment will want to creep in, but it is not helpful. Judging yourself or judging others is one of the biggest pitfalls I can warn you about on this journey. In being a financial guide, I have found that self-judgment is one of the biggest threats to experiencing true peace and prosperity. Forgiveness and appreciation are the greatest steadying principles I have found. When the winds blow and temperatures drop on the mountain – when the way forward seems treacherous – forgiveness and appreciation can be powerful defrosters.

It's one of the greatest gifts you can give yourself, to forgive.
Forgive everybody.

—Maya Angelou

Another workshop participant, Lynda, shared the effects of her money stress. "Growing up, my parents always argued about money. So, for question #4, I put 'In my family, money caused arguments.' I think that's probably the case for many people. What I didn't realize until just now was how this has affected my marriage." She took a deep breath. "It was really important to me to be married to someone who was good with money. So once I found the right person and married him, I let myself off the hook and didn't even think about money."

"We never had money conversations because I assumed that would just lead to arguments. I didn't want to argue with my husband. So I stuck my head in the sand. But he always persisted, wanting me to know about the investments and look at the statements with him and all that, and I felt so much resistance to these conversations. Let's be honest, I hated it! He thought he was being helpful, but it would always lead to an argument. I now realize that's because I was avoiding the topic, because I didn't want to argue!" She laughed ruefully. "Man. What was I doing?"

"Living out the story that was playing in your head," I said. "It makes sense once you tune in to the music. It's like a song that has been playing in the background all this time." I paused. She nodded. "And now," I proceeded gently, "you have the power to change the music if you choose. You can decide if you are tired of that old song and if so, you can tune in to something else – a different song that might better serve you both."

About a year later, she told me that this experience "saved her marriage." After learning more about finance in the rest of the workshop and gaining more confidence, she began to have conversations with her husband about their money situation. He was so excited that she showed interest in something he truly loved. Their relationship became much closer and more sincere than ever before.

Turning down the volume on our habitual, outdated, unhelpful money stories is NOT simply "fluff." It is deep, important, foundational work. It is essential. It is also what every successful person before you has had to face, and has done. And you can, too.

Just by having the courage to identify your money stories and tune in to your inner voices, you step out of darkness into the light. You now have the power to choose what stories and what voices you listen to. You can turn up the volume on your authentic inner voice—the most helpful and encouraging one. You can leave the baggage of the past behind and breathe the fresh air, see the clear sky, and know, or at least begin to believe, that you truly can climb this mountain.

This is big work. Take a moment to care for yourself. There is a bonus visualization activity in the *Peaceful Prosperity Workbook* to help you integrate this new information and give yourself a little love, if you'd like. Be sure to hug yourself and take a deep breath before moving on.

The Peaceful Prosperity Mindset: Foundation

I am braver than I believe, stronger than I seem, and smarter than I think.

I give myself grace when I make mistakes, remembering that I am always learning and mistakes are part of the learning process. I am gentle with myself.

I forgive myself for my past money behaviors and release myself from having to repeat any behaviors that do not serve me. I have a choice and a say in how I manage my money.

I allow myself to listen to my authentic self when I am making financial decisions. My authentic self supports me and lifts me up.

I let go of old beliefs about money. I allow myself to discover new tools, create new narratives, and open up to the idea that I can be financially successful.

I know, respect, and honor my goals. I know, respect, and honor my dreams. I know, respect, and honor the steps I am taking to bring my dreams to reality.

YOUR ASCENT: BUILDING MINDFUL BUDGETS

Peace is a daily, a weekly, a monthly process, gradually changing opinions, slowly eroding old barriers, quietly building new structures.

-*John F. Kennedy*

Chapter Two: The Invisible Column: Income

Chapter Three: The Troublesome Column: Expenses

Chapter Four: The Double-Edged Sword: Credit & Debt

My friend, you are living JFK's quote above.

In the last chapter, you showed the bravery to take a look at your opinions and possible barriers. That is going to help you "change those opinions" and "erode those old barriers."

Now let's work on "building new structures."

In this section, we begin the climb up your financial mountains. We'll start with familiar territory—places where most of us already have some experience and knowledge as we deal with the day-to-day aspects of money in our lives.

We're going to explore these areas with a fresh perspective now that we've dug down to the roots and rearranged our foundation in Chapter One. We're going to try to stay in that "beginner's mind" and look at these familiar areas with new eyes, minds, and hearts.

(And... spoiler alert! We may also have some fun.)

Let's go!

Chapter Two

The Invisible Column: Income

"If we did all the things we're capable of doing, we would literally astonish ourselves."

—*Thomas Edison*

W hat if I told you that you could focus on EXPANSION rather than deprivation when it comes to your budget?

If that seems like a bit of a stretch, stay with me.

Most people think about their expenses when they hear the word "budget." Budgeting and cutting back on spending are important – and we'll cover that in the next chapter. But looking only at expenses misses half of the equation. It's one way to change your money story, but it's not the only way.

Focusing only on the Expenses side of the budget is a HUGE blind spot. But it sure is an easy trap to fall into. After all, how many times a day are we wooed by words like "SALE,"

"SPECIAL DEAL," and "DISCOUNT"? We feel smart and powerful by knowing we have gotten the best price. We feel a thrill when we discover a secret "hack" to save money. And how many of us have done a spontaneous happy dance when we stack not one, not two, but THREE coupons? YES!!

These energetic jolts can be fun, but they can also cause us to get overly focused on our expenses. And if you focus on nothing but your expenses, you are neglecting half of your potential money power. It's like climbing up a mountain on one foot. It makes your journey longer and tougher than it needs to be. Allow me to invite you to shift your gaze just slightly, over to the Income side of the budget, and you will suddenly stand on both feet again. Your world will change completely.

Many people see income as one line on the budget sheet. "It's what I get from my employer," is often the thought, and that's about it. "I have to take that number and make it work." So most people get down to work slashing their expenses ruthlessly, getting them down as small as possible, to make that one income number work.

We all have multiple expenses, but what about multiple streams of income? Turning your attention to income helps you lean into this mind shift and expand your horizons significantly. Focusing on income leads you to ask different questions.

Instead of "How can I save more money?", you shift to asking, "How can I make more money?" This shifts your mindset from scarcity and fear to abundance and expansion. The powerful answer to the second question is this: increasing my income means I don't have to feel so guilty or afraid about spending money.

Think about it. If your income was larger, your expenses could expand as well. Another way of saying that is, by expanding your income side, you don't have as much pressure to contract on the expenses side. You give yourself more breathing room.

So first, let's give ourselves a little air to breathe. Let's start with the area that most people usually miss: the one that's hidden in plain sight. Let's start by exploring the invisible income column and allowing our vision to expand.

MULTIPLE STREAMS OF INCOME

Tom Corley, author of *Rich Habits* and *Change Your Habits, Change Your Life* surveyed hundreds of wealthy individuals and shared this observation: Unlike low-earning individuals, wealthier people

"...generated their income from multiple sources.

- 65 percent had three streams of income

- 45 percent had four streams of income

- 29 percent had five or more streams of income."

What a subtle yet significant difference! If you think of income as a stream and your bank account as a pool, you can see why having multiple streams feeding into your pool would be desirable. If one stream dries up, you're not headed for a deadly drought; there are other streams to help fill the pool. Think about all the reasons that one stream could dry up: getting laid off or fired, unexpected health issues, deciding to leave a job to raise children or help family – just to name a few. Multiple streams are far less risky than relying on only one stream.

So how do you develop multiple streams of income? Let's use the power of collective thinking to answer this question and get some ideas.

THE ART OF THE SIDE HUSTLE

Have you ever heard of a "side hustle"? Usually it means something you do on the side to make extra money. The term is a bit misleading, because I know some people whose "side hustle" has become their main income stream!

In the workshops at this point, we bring out a whiteboard and brainstorm side hustles together. I ask, "What are all the things you have heard of, that people have done to earn extra income?" No judging, just throwing them out there. We get to laugh, think creatively, and often be amazed by learning something new. Here are a few examples. I'm guessing you can probably add more.

- Babysitting / au pair / nanny.

- Eldercare or helping out an elderly person by running errands, etc.

- House-sitting – this one can allow you to live in places you'd never otherwise be able to experience. For example, one woman spent a month in Tuscany house-sitting for a wealthy friend.

- Dog walking or pet care – I know of a vet tech who runs a dog walking business on the weekends. It's a perfect gig for her because she loves dogs! She finds it easy and enjoyable. Since she has professional training, her customers trust her. Win-win. They find her service valuable and they are happy to pay her for it.

- Gardening or lawn care. Selling vegetables, preserves, or potpourri from the literal fruits of your labor.

- Odd jobs or handyman tasks like painting or repair.

- Housecleaning.

- Providing physical labor like help with moving, building IKEA furniture, running errands, etc. (TaskRabbit, Favor).

- Ride-sharing (Uber, Lyft).

- Renting out property like your house or a spare room (Airbnb, VRBO).

- Renting out your car (Hyrecar, Turo).

- Renting out your pool (yes, really! Check out Swimply).

- Selling goods to consignment shops – a great way to clean up your unused "stuff" that's languishing in your garage or storage unit, as well as make a little cash. This includes unwanted books you can sell to Half Price Books, for example, as well as unused furniture and clothing.

- Selling all kinds of goods on Etsy, Craigslist, Facebook, or eBay – I know many women who have a craft or hobby they love that they have turned into a side hustle this way. One of them makes jewelry and funny T-shirts. She has a blast and picks up a couple of extra bucks on the side.

- Responding to surveys / being a secret shopper – this can involve going to a store or working from your home computer and not leaving your house at all.

- Posting videos, blog posts, or other social media content online and receiving revenues or commissions.

- Providing professional services – like editing, writing, proofreading, graphic design, resume writing, calligraphy, accounting, or bookkeeping – the list is extensive! You can check out online markets to see what is out there (Fiverr, Upwork, Redbubble, for example).

- Providing creative services like recording anything from meditations to original music; becoming a voiceover artist or audiobook reader. I know of a painter who does personalized murals in children's rooms.

- Part-time work like tutoring or teaching English as a second language (Wyzant) or being a virtual assistant (HireMyMom).

This list is far from exhaustive. A few minutes on an internet search can be eye-opening to the possibilities that are out there. Or better yet, ask your friends and family! The possibilities seem to be endless!

"If you hear a voice within you say, 'you cannot paint,' then by all means paint, and that voice will be silenced."

—*Vincent Van Gogh*

You may be thinking, "Laura, I can't do any of that! I don't have any special skills!" If so, let me tell you a story.

In the 2017 movie *Jumanji: Welcome to the Jungle* (have you seen this version with Jack Black? How he embodies the attitude of a spoiled teenage girl is priceless and worth the watch if you haven't seen it. But I digress.) — four characters are thrown into a game and must work through a series of challenges to make their way back home. One of the first tasks they are given is to figure out where they are and where they are going. They are provided with a map to do so, but three of the characters can't see anything on the map. They discover that only one of them has the skill of cartography which allows him to read the map. It turns out that each of them has a set of skills and strengths (as well as some humorous weaknesses) that they can only access by looking within. The characters realize they must work together using their various talents to solve the riddles, get through the game, and successfully get to the top of the mountain.

Like these characters, each of us has strengths that we cannot see; skills that can get us to the top of the mountain only after we uncover them. I am certain you probably have skills, knowledge, and talents that come so naturally to you that you don't even think about them. Maybe your friends compliment you on these skills, and you answer, "Yeah, but anybody can do that!" Well, that's likely not the case, or your friends wouldn't have taken notice of your skills.

Let's turn our attention to those skills now. Consider the question: "What's your superpower?" If it's truly difficult to see yourself this way, pretend as if you are describing a friend instead of yourself. Or, you can actually ask a friend this question and have them tell you what amazing qualities you possess. In the *Peaceful Prosperity Workbook*, there's a "Transferable Skills" exercise that leads you through a journal exercise to help you discover them and how they can help you financially.

Opportunities Where You Least Expect Them

My friend Anna decided to become a Pampered Chef consultant many years ago. She wasn't even interested in cooking at the time! But her husband encouraged her to go to a friend's Pampered Chef party and reluctantly, she went. After all, she wanted to be nice to her friend.

At the party, the consultant was making a delicious lemon dessert using a simple recipe. Her aim was to illustrate how easy it was to bake when using Pampered Chef products. Halfway through the demonstration, someone pointed out that the consultant had forgotten to put in the main ingredient: lemon! Quickly assessing the situation, the consultant added the missing ingredient and went on, not flustered a bit. She reassured all in attendance that the dessert would taste fine. The lemon treat did indeed taste wonderful, and Anna's eyes were opened to a new world. If baking didn't have to be precise and intimidating, she could do it!

Empowered by this new experience, Anna went on to make sale after sale as a Pampered Chef consultant. She paid off her credit card (her original goal). Then she moved on to something she had always dreamed of, but never had the money to do: she was able to publish her first book.

Now Anna runs a successful publishing company that allows others to achieve this dream (including yours truly). And it all started with a lemon dessert and putting her heart into an unexpected opportunity.

Thoughts on Multi-Level Marketing (MLM)

Companies like Mary Kay, Avon, Pampered Chef, Tupperware – and I'm sure many others – have made it possible to potentially make money by directly selling products to others (family, friends), as well as receiving a commission when you recruit others to begin selling "under" you. These are all legitimate companies where I have seen people become successful in setting up a business. If the idea of making money in this way appeals to you, be careful, however, not to fall into the trap of a "pyramid scheme."

The key difference between "MLM" and a "pyramid scheme" is that a pyramid scheme provides bigger bonuses for recruitment over product sales. In other words, more (or all) of the money is made by recruiting new people into the program rather than selling actual products. Pyramid schemes are considered a scam by the Federal Trade Commission (FTC). They can look like MLMs, so it's always a good idea to do your homework before signing up. The FTC has good articles on what to look out for, as does the Securities and Exchange Commission (SEC). I suggest you do an internet search to locate these resources on the FTC and/or SEC websites.

Important Questions

For any "side hustle" you are eager to delve into, it's important to ask questions and set up expectations from the start. This can mean the difference between a successful side business and a frustrating money pit.

The first thing to keep in mind is: you never want a side hustle to become an expensive hobby rather than a source of INCOME! So you'll want to ask questions like these up front:

- How much can I expect to earn from this? How many hours per week are required?

- What do I need to get started (e.g., equipment, supplies, or training)? Do I have this already? (For example, the vet tech, who already had training with dogs, provided pet services.) Or do I know someone I could barter with?

- Finding mentors is a great idea here. Do you know someone who is doing this already? Are they making money? Can you reach out to them and find out what it's like? (If you don't have any potential mentors yet, it is easier than ever to research an idea, read reviews, and find out answers to these questions.)

You can use the worksheet in the *Peaceful Prosperity Workbook* to help you organize your research.

Giving Your Side Hustle a Purpose

When I was in college, I took a part-time job working at Pier One Imports. It was my dream to spend a semester studying abroad in London, England. Armed only with that dream, I attended an informational session about study abroad programs and I made notes. I asked the counselors about all the costs and wrote them down. I added estimates for food and fun money. Ultimately I came up with an amount that would allow me to make my dream a reality.

Then I worked backward and looked at my choices. If I made $X/per hour at my job, I would need to work a total of X hours to get to my goal. I could decide if I wanted to work two 8-hour shifts every weekend or four 4-hour shifts in the evenings, etc. I talked to my boss and we set up a schedule. I was on my way.

Every time a grumpy customer gave me a hard time, I would think of my trip to England. I imagined what it was going to be like to bite into freshly fried fish and chips on the Thames pier, how my footsteps would echo on the cobblestone streets where Dickens had walked, and what the rose garden of Kensington Palace would look like in the spring. Then I would smile at the grumpy customer and think to myself conspiratorially, "I have a secret you don't know about. I'm going to England!"

If I hadn't had that very specific goal, and very specific ideas – smells, sights, sounds – to go along with it, I wouldn't have felt very motivated in my work at Pier One. I wouldn't have enjoyed my work as much as I did. At times, it would have been a real bummer.

But it wasn't because that side job had a specific purpose. It was more than just a job. It was the way I was going to get my dream. You can tolerate a lot of small annoyances when you are working towards something truly significant to you.

The Mysterious Ceiling

For all of our research and planning to expand our income, we may still run into invisible walls and find it frustrating to make any progress. That doesn't mean we need to give up. Nope, it just means we may have hit our "earnings ceiling."

Remember the wily evil wizard Saruman from Lord of the Rings? Just like him, our earnings ceiling can infiltrate our minds so cleverly that we don't even notice it. Or worse, we can believe the whisperings that tell us, "You are trapped! That's just the way it is." It's a terrifying thought. As long as we believe this is true, there can be no peace of mind, and making any progress can be difficult.

But what if it's not true? What if you can make more money than you think you can? Are you even open to that possibility?

The "Discover Your Earnings Ceiling" exercise by Karen McCall invites you to use your imagination to explore this question. The exercise lists varying amounts of annual income and asks you to picture your life, thoughts, and feelings at each level. It is an eye-opening experience. Karen's worksheet is included in the *Peaceful Prosperity Workbook* and I invite you to do it now to see what you learn about yourself.

What most people find is that, as the levels increase, their emotions move from fear to comfort and back to fear again. Where this shift happens is very personal. It may be related to your past work experience or to your money beliefs that we explored in Chapter One. It may be something you were taught as a child or young adult, or something you read or heard about more recently.

Wherever it comes from, I don't want you to think your earnings ceiling is necessarily problematic. It is simply a valuable piece of information about yourself.

Jessica described this part of the workshop as "a thrilling mental exercise: scary and fun and I learned a lot!" She realized she had always made just under her earnings ceiling amount. She felt frustrated that she couldn't make more. She blamed her job, her boss, her family, and society at large. These were probably all true factors operating in her life.

However, once she saw what her earnings ceiling was, she felt the desire to break through it. No longer was it something she had to accept; it was something she could control.

The knowledge she gained from the "Discover Your Earnings Ceiling" exercise emboldened her to consider asking for a raise at work.

She prepared her case and practiced it. When she finally presented it to her boss, to her great surprise, her request was granted—without any hesitation. This lead her to ask, "Why wasn't I given a raise before?" Her boss replied simply, "You never asked."

OTHER WAYS OF EXPANDING YOUR INCOME

This brings us to an important point. Side hustles are fun to consider, but let's not neglect your current income stream. How do you currently make money? For many people, it is either from an employer (W-2 income) or from a business (1099 income). Either way, it's worth asking how you could potentially increase that income stream—the one that is already flowing. After all, it's probably not set in stone. With a little help, it could probably increase, too. Let's look at how.

If You Have a Boss

Negotiating a raise with your employer often feels tricky... risky, even. What if the answer to your request isn't only, "No, we can't do that," but also includes "and PS, you're fired!" Yikes. It's important to be able to handle this gracefully.

Thankfully, there are plenty of books and blogs on the subject that can help you prepare and rehearse. Here are the key pointers that I hear from women who have done this successfully (like Jessica):

- Do your homework: get familiar with the company hierarchy, culture, and financial health. Research the current salary rates for your role, both inside and outside of the company.

- Know your worth: be able to talk about your accomplishments (specific tasks and dates achieved are especially good), what you have contributed, and what you will contribute (skills, enthusiasm, experience) to the company in the future.

- Ask for what you want. This is what Jessica learned. After doing all the other parts so well, it was an easy "yes" for her boss to agree to what she asked for. The reason she hadn't gotten a raise already wasn't due to her performance or issues at the company; it was because she had never realized her worth. She also had never spoken up for what she wanted.

- Keep an open mind and be flexible. Perhaps other factors play into the company's decisions about pay increases that you are unaware of. Try not to take decisions personally. Instead, come up with a backup plan. If a raise is not in the cards for whatever reason, perhaps you can ask for a more flexible work schedule or time off instead. After all, more time off could equal more time to develop your side hustle!

If You Are the Boss

When you are an entrepreneur, you set your own prices and have more control over how and what you are paid. I love working with entrepreneurs because they are usually passionately involved with every aspect of their business, from creation to delivery. They take pride in their work. But even the most passionate entrepreneur may experience hesitation when it comes to money. That's natural because it's often difficult for us to think about charging for something we love doing so much that we'd likely do it for free! What we don't realize is that if or when we do this, we're actually robbing those we serve and doing them a disservice, not a favor.

I once helped a middle-aged man plan for his retirement. It was a fun activity for both of us, going through his various retirement accounts, building a plan for how he was going to distribute his money, and creating a lifestyle post-paycheck that was going to be fulfilling and highly satisfying.

When we finished our work, he asked me for the bill. I knew from having worked with him for several weeks that he was quite a frugal man. Sheepishly, I handed over the invoice for the hours I had worked on his plan. I think I may have even avoided eye contact. I was so ashamed to hand him a bill at all.

There was silence for a moment as he read the invoice. Then he said, "Laura, my dear. You are not charging enough. The value of what you have done for me is far greater than this." I looked up and saw that he was actually distressed. His hand hovered over his checkbook as if he were conflicted about what to do. And I thought he would push back about the money, and that I would have to renegotiate the price for him. I was so wrong!

This taught me two very important things. First, we tend to seriously undervalue ourselves and the work we do for others. It's hard for any of us to see ourselves clearly, and it's especially difficult when we add our layers of money baggage and money stories that can cloud our vision.

Second, human beings crave reciprocity. If you do something really outstanding for me, chances are, I want to show my appreciation by doing something equally nice for you. If I can't show you appreciation in some way—if I am unable to reciprocate—then I feel awful. In the case of this gentleman, his hesitation and distress were saying, "I don't really have any other method to show you my appreciation other than giving you money for your service. Please help me close the reciprocity loop by allowing me to pay you a fair trade!"

From then on, I was more mindful of my pricing. I researched and asked other financial planners what they charged. I allowed my clients to tell me where they found value. I put on my earmuffs and didn't listen to those "foul voices on the air" that had kicked up in my mind and told me I shouldn't be charging for my work. I tuned in to the more truthful voices of my trusted clients and experienced friends and let them guide me instead.

Finally... The Myth of Passive Income

Wouldn't it be nice if you could "make money while you sleep?" If somehow you didn't have to do much, but could still make a lot of money? This is the siren-song of many "passive income" strategies, but don't get lured in... you could crash upon the rocks.

The IRS says "passive income" comes from two sources: either rental property or a business in which you do not actively participate, such as being paid royalties or dividends. Does this sound familiar?

Many people think that royalties, for example, would be a great source of passive income. "If only I could write that award-winning book / song / etc." The truth is, even after the creative muse has spoken and you have captured the magic, it requires a heck of a lot of work to get your wonderful creation out into the world. The people have to find it. And be willing to pay for it. This might not be what you imagine when you hear the term "passive income."

Rental income is also envisioned as a wonderful passive income stream: you buy a property, turn around and rent it out, and collect the rent checks. What could be easier? Ask any property manager about the reality of being a landlord, and they will tell you it is an ongoing job, not "passive" by any means.

Finally, let's talk about dividends. We will get into investments more later, but it's worth bringing up here that dividend investing is also often heralded as an ideal way to make money without doing very much. "Just put your money into blue chip dividend stocks" is something I often hear. This certainly can be a way to create an income stream—but it requires patience and persistence. I don't have to tell you that stock values go up and down, and for some, that may be nerve-racking. It is a viable way to make money, but it is not without its angst, which the term "passive" seems to imply.

This is certainly not to discourage you from trying out these ways of making income if they appeal to you. Instead, I offer you these observations for two reasons: first, to reiterate the importance and value of looking into what is involved in any new way of making income before you jump in. As much as possible, you want to go in with your eyes open and with reasonable expectations for the outcome. The second reason is to empower you with knowledge so that you can make better choices and experience better control over your income. I like to think of knowledge as a suit of armor—it helps to protect you from the arrows of ignorance.

"Knowledge is power...knowledge is safety...knowledge is happiness."

-Thomas Jefferson

The Peaceful Prosperity Mindset: Income

I am enthusiastic to learn new ways of thinking about money. Instead of focusing on my expenses and feeling scarcity, I focus on creating multiple streams of income and feeling expansion.

I am optimistic about my financial future. I am confident in my ability to make money.

I have talents and unique skills that are valuable to others. I can tap into these hidden treasures to help me expand my income.

I know how to do research and make informed decisions about my money opportunities. This helps me to move forward with confidence.

I know my earnings ceiling and how that may have held me back in the past. I give myself permission to move beyond my ceiling.

I am important and give myself permission to experience financial success. I allow myself to speak up about my worth. I allow others to express their appreciation of my work through money.

CONGRATS! You Are Crafting a New 3-Legged Stool

Back when I was first learning about finance, I remember hearing the term "three-legged stool." It was a term used to describe the three things that everyone must have for a successful retirement. Those three things were: Social Security, Personal Savings, and Investments. The image was, if you have these three things, you have a stable stool that will provide financial stability, resulting in peace and happiness in your "golden years."

Over time as I worked with people on building their financial futures, I came to observe that this setup wasn't quite how the peaceful, happy retirees had accomplished their financial goals. Rather, their three-legged stool relied upon different "legs": Business, Real Estate, and Investments. It was an observation that struck me.

Perhaps these three legs may sound completely foreign to you. But do you realize that by thinking about a side hustle, as you have done here, you are already building the "business" part of the successful person's three-legged stool? I wonder what else you can do and perhaps surprise yourself?

"It's a great thing when you realize you still have the ability to surprise yourself. Makes you wonder what else you can do that you've forgotten about."

– Alan Ball

Okay, NOW you are ready to look at your expenses! If you feel empowered, as I hope you do now, my guess is that you'll look at your expenses differently.

Chapter Three

The Troublesome Column: Expenses

"Change your language and you change your thoughts."
—Karl Albrecht

There's an old story about a traveler back in the Middle Ages who came across two bricklayers one day. He watched as each of the workers performed their hard labor.

He asked the first worker, who seemed to be struggling, "What are you doing?" The bricklayer turned to him with a sour face and moaned, "I am picking up these heavy bricks, straining my back, then throwing cement between them. It gets all over my sleeves and makes a mess. Then I bang down my hammer in hopes that they'll stay where I put them, which they never do. And finally, I'm walking through all this mud to go get more bricks, and do it all over again! It's the worst job ever." And the worker slumped away to get more bricks.

The traveler then turned to the other bricklayer. He appeared to be doing the same job, but he was smiling as he did so. Curious as to what was different for this man, the traveler asked, "And what are you doing?" The second bricklayer turned his face up to the traveler and beamed from the mud. He said, "I am building a cathedral!"

When you are in the "mud" of your finances, it can be easy to focus on the inconveniences and drudgery. It can be really challenging to remember that you are building something beautiful that you should feel proud of. Our next exercise is going to help us bring meaning to the mundane. We'll do this by working with both numbers and words.

Let's start with the words and consider the language of budgeting. How can we look at this work as building a cathedral, rather than hauling bricks?

On a usual expense report, you'll find categories such as:

- "Rent/Mortgage Payment"

- "Utilities"

- "Federal Income Taxes"

- "Health Insurance"

- "Child Care"

- "Car Payment."

Does anyone want to change the language here? To many people, these terms feel like bricks. Some of you might be perfectly comfortable with these labels. And that's fine. This is YOUR list. But some of you might have a negative reaction to the term "Rent/Mortgage Payment." And I know a lot of people don't feel particularly enthused about "Federal Income Taxes." So how do we make these budget categories feel less burdensome and more, dare I say it, fun?

Let's start by considering a change to the language. What if, instead of "Rent/Mortgage Payment," we were to call that "Home"? How about "Sanctuary"? Or what about "love shack"? Who's to say we can't?

And what if, instead of "Utilities," we called this, "My warm morning shower" or "Keeping the lights on"?

Can you feel how – just by changing our words – we can create a new mindset and attitude? I love this part of workshop because it always gets the creative juices flowing! New terms spring to life, some poetic and flowery; some practical, but all with rich, meaningful stories behind them.

For example, I have heard the term "Car Payment" become everything from "Freedom Mobile" and "Stylin Wheels" to "Safe Transport" and "Mommy Van."

"Groceries" can be renamed "Nourishment" or "Healthy Food."

"Child Care" transformed into "Emancipated Parents" for one couple.

"Pet Expenses" changed to "My Fuzzy Angel" for another woman.

"Insurance" has often been relabeled as "Peace of Mind" or "Security."

"Emergency Fund" can become "Ooops!" or "Life Happens" or "Curve Ball" or (my favorite) "Plot Twist!"

One woman switched her "Spotify subscription" to "Life Soundtrack." Use your imagination.

This should be fun, but some categories can be challenging. For example, I have noticed that the category of "self-care" stops some women. Bethany realized this in one workshop, saying, "I have always been meticulous with my budget. I have multiple savings accounts and I try to do everything right. But I realized that I've just been spinning my wheels with all my savings. I never spend it on anything. I realized just now that I have wanted a massage for three years, but I've never allowed myself to have one! Now that "self-care" is an item on my expense sheet, it feels like I have permission to do it. In fact, it seems silly NOT to!" (The other women in the class applauded her, by the way.) Do you need to add "self-care" to your expenses list?

Rachel had the epiphany that the category "Eating Out" meant something very different than she had originally assumed. She explained in the workshop:

"I always felt really guilty about eating out. Like, I'm capable of making my own food! Why should I pay more to have someone else make it for me? What a waste!"

"I felt wrong for loving to eat out. But just now I realized something. For me, it's not about the food. I'm an extrovert and I thrive on other people's energy. For me, eating out is Socializing Time! And that is so much more important to me than the food or even the money. It feeds my soul and makes me happy. It gives me the energy to do other things I need to do. It will still be an occasional splurge, I think, and not a habit. But now that I realized this significance, I won't feel so bad about eating out. I would even go so far as to put it in my Personal Mental Health category! But I think I will call it "Connection" for now, to remind me of what it does for my spirit."

Sharon had a similar shift in her relationship with the expense category "Student Loan Payment." She said she always hated that category and dreaded making the payments. It was more than feeling ashamed about having a large debt. "Whenever I looked at it, I felt hateful and triggered," she said. "There's so much emotional baggage from my college years. I thought my parents would help financially more than they did, but after grad school, I realized that no one was coming to rescue me. I was resentful and just wanted it to go away. So I pretended it wasn't there."

I asked Sharon about what she studied and she lit up. As she shared stories about the experiences she had in college, she seemed to soften. "I guess they were some really great years, and they made me what I am today. For that, I am extremely grateful." She was quiet for a few moments. "In that case," she said slowly, "I guess I'm glad I did it. I'm glad I went to college. I guess I could look at that payment and remember what it allowed me to do, which I wouldn't have done otherwise."

A smile came across her face. "I'm going to rename it "Mind Expansion" to honor my experience. And then you know what? I don't think I will resent paying it anymore. I actually feel grateful."

Other types of debt can be renamed to shine a positive light on the experience as well. I have heard medical debt reframed as "Healing Adventure." Divorce expenses were renamed as "Life Pivot." Travel bills were renamed "My Big Fat Italian Experience." The new name helped a woman remember why she had those high credit card payments that she disliked. Bringing to mind the warm sunny beaches and delicious food she experienced helped her to lessen her resentment for the bills. Ironically, this motivated her to pay them off faster. She said the new name planted a seed of inspiration that whispered: "Maybe I can do that again when I get this paid off..."

Even taxes, a category which is often distasteful, can be reframed in a more positive light. For example, Cathy shared a story about this which changed my mind forever.

"I'm a good citizen and of course I pay my taxes," she started. "And I never used to particularly enjoy paying my taxes—like everybody. But then one night, many years ago, my brother had a heart attack while he was at my house. As you can imagine, I panicked. But I remembered to call 911. Help was on the way. As I tried to make him comfortable and do what I could, I just kept telling myself through the fear and distress, 'It will all be okay when they get here. It will all be okay when they get here.' You have never seen anyone so grateful to hear ambulance sirens. The ambulance guys took him off to the hospital and he was fine, eventually. But I tell you, I never felt so thankful in all my life. And now it dawned on me: I will never resent paying my taxes again!"

Bari Tessler, in her book, *The Art of Money*, says:

"The simple act of renaming our budget categories can be transformative. It's a small thing, and might even seem petty

or silly, but renaming can connect us with the personal value of our expenses. No longer are "my life" and "those cold, dusty numbers" living in separate rooms: your bookkeeping system reveals and strengthens their intimate connection and reminds you of it on a regular basis."

Bari further suggests that you "reframe, rename, and reimagine your expense categories at will." You don't need to rename everything, of course. If "mortgage" feels okay to you, then leave it for now. But at least try renaming some categories. Think of it as a mental exercise.

What might it feel like to find a more playful or meaningful name for your expense categories? You can use the *Peaceful Prosperity Workbook* to get creative.

Remember, there are no wrong answers. Find a word or phrase that resonates for you and write it down. After all, this is YOUR list. Own it.

At this point, you're probably eager to get into some numbers, so let's do it!

Now that you have new names for your expense categories, let's write in rough estimates for each category. Do this

BEFORE you go and look them up. You may know some categories to the penny, or you may have no idea. If you don't know for sure, that's okay. Take your best guess. Write in something for every line—even the vaguest idea you have now. If you get stuck, say to yourself: "It's okay that I don't know. What's my best guestimate?"

The key here is to free your mind. Think: "there are no wrong answers at this time. These are just guesses." We will go back and update them later. Right now, it's more important to have the courage to wander into the unknown and approach your numbers with a sense of curiosity rather than rigidity. And besides, it's quite possible you will have more correct guesses than you think.

After you have given your best guess in every category, I'd like you to do two things. First, step back and take a break. Second, pat yourself on the back.

Smile. Sigh. Maybe do a little dance. (It's okay, no one is looking.) Do something to show yourself a little appreciation for what you've just done. You are making huge progress!

Once you have given yourself a little appreciation and celebration, you are ready to go on and retrieve your actual numbers. This means digging into your checking account statements and credit card statements.

As you do this, please remember: these numbers do not define you. They tell you a story of behaviors and patterns. And now, that's a story that you can begin to change.

When you're done, you should have an Expenses sheet that includes all of your expense categories in a list like this:

- New Name (i.e., Love Shack)

- Estimate / Guess Amount

- Actual Amount

You have just created a mighty tool for creating your financial freedom!

To illustrate how powerful this is, let's go back to our mountain climbing analogy. By going through this budget exercise, you have reached the first peak. From here, you can see from a new vantage point. Often people will say to me, "I had no idea I was spending so much on THAT! Why am I doing that? It's not even that important to me! I'm going to cut that back..." Knowledge, my friend, is power.

As you look at your budget with new clarity, you are empowered to make better decisions. Maybe you discontinue an old gym membership that you haven't used in a while. Maybe there are other subscriptions that you forgot you had. It may take a little legwork to find out how to cancel these outdated expenses, but it is worth your time. Even if the subscription doesn't take up a large part of your budget, just the fact that you are clearing out the old makes way for the new. And that's a good feeling.

Now let's get down to some specific budgeting strategies.

"A budget is telling your money where to go instead of wondering where it went."

—John C. Maxwell

BUDGET OPTIONS

Being mindful of where your money is going can make you stronger, happier, and in a better position to achieve your life goals. How you do it is important, but don't get stuck thinking there is a right or a wrong way.

There are many ways to set up a budget, and there are pros and cons to each method. The key is to have the right amount of *flexibility* in your budget so that you can maintain *consistency* with it. Even if your budget method is mathematically brilliant, if it's difficult to follow, you won't stick to it for long.

Here are four popular budgeting techniques worth considering:

Pay Yourself First

Well-known financial author David Bach says traditional budgets tend to fail because they are too restrictive and go against human nature. Traditional budgeting requires you to tell yourself that you "can't" spend money on things you enjoy because you have to pay everyone else first. Bach says a better approach is to start by "paying yourself first." In his opinion, doing this feels less restrictive and more enjoyable. That means you'll stick with it longer.

- The first priority of "paying yourself first" is putting money into your retirement accounts, investments, and savings. At least 10-20% of your income should go here. Bach goes further, saying that if you want to be average, save 5-10% of your income; if you want to be rich, save 15-20% of your income; and if you want to retire early, save more than 20% of your income into your retirement accounts.

- After savings, next comes your life necessities like rent/mortgage, utilities, insurance, and debt payments.

- Last comes the category of lifestyle, like food and

entertainment.

Bach suggests that this type of budgeting helps you to feel more in control, especially if you put the top priority payments on "autopilot." In other words, set up automatic deductions from your paycheck to your retirement accounts and investments. Use your bank's online bill pay to automate deposits to your savings accounts. This helps you to build a better financial future consistently, rather than letting life's busyness get in the way. Bach says the "I'll do it someday..." mentality is the way to guarantee being poor.

The 50-20-30 Rule

Touted by LearnVest, this method has gained popularity in recent years. This method simplifies budgeting by having you direct your monthly after-tax (take-home) pay into three areas:

- 50% goes toward necessities (food, shelter, utilities, and minimum debt payments),

- 20% goes toward long-term financial priorities (retirement, nest egg for a house, and/or any additional payments to debt), and

- 30% goes toward desires (vacation, entertainment, pets, hobbies, and other non-necessities).

The definition of each of these categories allows for a small amount of "wiggle room." (i.e. is your cell phone a "necessity" or a "desire"? You decide.) At the same time, the percentages aim to keep your financial focus in the "right" areas (you'll notice that more goes towards necessities than desires).

The Splurge Bucket Variation

Remit Sethi, author of *I Will Teach You to Be Rich*, breaks down the 50-20-30 rule a bit further. He suggests that a "top-down budget" (where you write down what you should spend) is better than a "bottom-up budget" (where you write down what you did spend). This is because a top-down budget lets you set goals, which creates motivation rather than restriction (echoing David Bach's advice). Here's Sethi's suggested budget breakdown:

- 50-60% to necessities including debt and insurance payments,

- 10% to investments like 401(k)'s, IRAs, and Roth IRAs,

- 5-10% to savings for gifts, a future vacation, house nest egg, etc.,

- 20-35% to "guilt-free spending" on your one splurge like eating out, clothing, movies, etc.

This is perhaps the most flexible budgeting method, because it allows for varying spending ranges, rather than requiring strict percentages be maintained. Sethi's method also acknowledges human nature by creating a "splurge" bucket. Contrary to what you might think, having a specific category for splurges just might help to keep them in check, rather than get out of control.

The F.I.R.E. Variation

Popularized by Vicki Robin and Joe Dominguez in 1992 when they published the book *Your Money or Your Life*, F.I.R.E. means "Financially Independent Retire Early." This one is hard-core but fascinating. The basic premise is to save 50-70% of what you take home, living way below your means. The goal is to achieve financial independence in about 10 years, long before most traditional budgeting plans allow.

I have found that this strict system can be modified to something more moderate and still help you get ahead significantly. My husband and I have gamified this. Each year, we figure out how much income we expect to make. Then, we calculate what 30- 50% of that income would be. We take a deep breath, then dig into our budget to try to come up with a way to hit that 50% savings number. True confession: we almost never do. (Or at least, not yet!) BUT, by doing this exercise, we have been able to hit the 30-35% range most years.

And that's WAY more than we would have saved if we had not been paying attention.

The point of showing you several different ways to budget is to help you bust the myth that there is ONE correct way to budget (and the belief that you are probably doing it "wrong"). In fact, there are certainly more than these four approaches, but for the sake of simplicity, I wanted to highlight the most popular that I have seen.

Bonus: If you and your partner / spouse / child are arguing over how to budget, perhaps realizing that there is more than one way to do it can help you reach common ground and move forward successfully. Remember, no matter where you are in your financial life, there's always room to grow and learn and improve your situation!

Let's go back to the power of collective thinking. Have you heard of other creative ways to budget? Here are some smart budgeting ideas I have heard of or used:

- Driving used cars

- Buying used goods (furniture, clothing, even electronics) at secondhand stores

- Searching for coupons or promo/discount codes before making an internet purchase (there are tons of these! Just try searching "discount code for..." and see what you can find.)

- Cutting cable television service completely (do you really watch it that much?)

- Renegotiating your internet/cell phone bill

- Using credit card points for travel (more on this in the next chapter)

- Using credit card rewards for gift cards (birthdays, holidays)

- Lowering eating out expenses by using restaurant rewards and loyalty programs; only ordering water; and/or skipping desserts and appetizers.

- Comparison shopping (there are apps for this like Honey which tell you where you can buy the same item for less. Also, some stores like Best Buy have a price match guarantee if you ask.)

- Cutting or eliminating education expenses by volunteering at your child's school

- Bartering (e.g., one friend got handyman work done in exchange for teaching him how to create a podcast)

- Holding potlucks or picnics with friends or family; everyone contributes instead of one person paying for catering.

These are just a few ideas! You probably know more. Who in your life can you ask that might have other great budgeting ideas?

KNOW WHY YOU BUY

"Too many people spend money they earned... to buy things they don't want... to impress people that they don't like."

— Will Rogers

Workshop attendee Daphne wrote a beautiful description of an epiphany she had about her spending habits, which I think is powerful and helpful. She asked me to share it with you here.

When I decided to quit my job and become a freelancer, I had to curtail my spending – and by *a lot*. One of the questions I started asking myself every time I wanted to buy something was "Do I *really* need that?" And by "need" I mean: would I die of hunger, be naked, homeless, or sick if I didn't purchase the item? Of course, I bought lots of items that didn't strictly fit that definition of "need," but by asking the question, it got me to start thinking more critically about need vs. want.

If I wanted to purchase something that wasn't strictly a need, I would then ask myself WHY I wanted the item. Was it for convenience? Because it was pretty? Because it would make *me* look pretty? Because everyone else had one? As I began to drill down with the questions, I often discovered that I was uncomfortable with the answers I was discovering.

Sometimes I wanted to purchase an item because it not only made me feel attractive, but because I felt so unattractive that I was looking for *anything* that would make me feel more attractive. Sometimes I wanted to purchase an item because I thought it might make me look smarter. In my own mind, I *knew* I wasn't smart, so if some item could make me *appear* smart, then I felt I needed that thing. Sometimes I wanted to purchase an item because it would make me feel good about myself in general. My sense of never being good enough led me to desire a lot of items that simply cluttered up my home in my quest to feel that I was "good enough."

Besides understanding the specific "why's" of my own buying habits, I discovered the most insidious issue of all for me: shopping as a numbing agent. When I had a lucrative job, I could buy a lot of stuff and it wasn't a financial problem. But my house was full of stuff that I just *had* to have at the time and my closets were full of stuff that I would later be surprised to find that I owned.

Because I shopped at discount stores, the money I saved made me think I was being smart, but it wasn't until I ran out of money that I realized how shopping had become a drug for me. I discovered that I couldn't even go into the grocery store without wanting to buy something that I didn't need.

Facing my spending "why's" was painful, but when I realized that shopping was more of an activity to help me fill an emotional hole than to solve a physical problem, I could focus my attention on *healing* that hole, instead of filling it with a never-ending stream of meaningless stuff. When I healed my hole enough to stop the money drain, there was a rather unexpected bonus: I found the time, money, and energy to focus on what *really* mattered to me in life.

Can you relate? Daphne's experience is significant, but it is not unusual. Allison had a similar experience which she shared with me months after our workshop. I ran into her at the grocery store and I asked her how it was going. "Great!" she said, almost a bit surprised by her honest exclamation.

"I've paid off my credit card and next year I'll have my house paid off!"

"Wow!" I said. "How'd you do all that?"

"It's funny," she said in wonder. "I don't feel like I've done anything differently. What is different is my attitude toward spending. See, in the classes, I remembered that my dad always spent freely on us kids as we were growing up. Nothing was too good for his children. So I connected the dots and realized, that's how I feel about spending money: it's an expression of love. It came from my dad, but I realized that's what I was doing. It's why I was spending money on things I didn't even need. When I felt down, I went and spent money on myself, and that's what made me feel better, like I was loved."

She smiled through misty eyes. "But Dad's gone now. So I talked to myself, and I said, 'You have your dad's love, you always will. You don't need to do anything to get that.' And now I just don't feel the need to spend as much anymore. I'm happy. I also feel closer to Dad."

Maybe now is a good time to reflect on the Digging Deep activity from Chapter One, or reflect and journal on the reasons you spend money like Daphne and Allison did. Just ask yourself, why do you buy?

Once you have given that a little thought, let's turn to another important question: Why do you save?

Savings Buckets

"A man who spends and saves money is the happiest man, because he has both enjoyments."

—*Samuel Johnson*

Many people start with their expenses and then save what is left. You can do that, and you can create a successful budget. But, as David Bach pointed out, there is another way. I have observed that women who get ahead in life and accomplish surprising and wonderful things are the ones who think about budgeting differently: they think about *saving* before they think about *spending*.

Take Diane, for example. Early in her career in the medical field, she decided that she wanted to buy a house. But she didn't want to wait around for years (or for a rich husband). She wanted to own a home sooner rather than later. Diane wanted a house so badly that she talked about it all the time to her friends. They dared her to do it because they thought it was an impossible goal.

This lit a fire under Diane.

She figured out how much money she would need for a down payment on a home in her area. Then she took that amount and figured out how much she would need to save per month if she wanted to reach her goal in three years. She was so motivated that she entered that as an item in her budget and treated it as non-negotiable. House savings came first. What she had left after saving was what she had available to spend.

Two years and ten months later, you should have seen the faces of Diane's friends when she purchased her home. They told her, "Hey, that's not fair!" They told her she was crazy. And she laughed and said, "That may be true, but I have a house now and that's what I wanted."

I believe that what helped Diane to reach her goal was not only exercising great spending control but also getting super-specific about what she was saving for and WHY. This focus allowed her to ramp up her savings and keep up the pace she set for herself. She also had a very specific timeframe, so she knew she would not have to maintain her restrictive budget forever.

Let's talk about how you can put this to work in your budget. Ask yourself a simple question. What are you saving for?

Maybe you want to take a vacation with your family to Greece.

Maybe you want to expand and modernize your tiny kitchen.

Maybe you want to help fund education for a child.

Maybe you want to be sure you have enough money if a medical need arises.

Maybe you want to buy a motorcycle.

Whatever it is, you probably have several financial goals in your mind. Take a moment now to jot them down. There's a page in the *Peaceful Prosperity Workbook* for you to do this, or you may use your own journal or a piece of paper.

Then, take another moment to flesh out each goal you have listed and give it life. Engaging all your senses is key. How does it look, smell, and taste? Who are you with? What does it sound like? You might even consider including visual representations of your goals. You can include drawings or photos alongside your descriptions, or create a vision board.

Whatever method you choose, refer to this list often. Put it in your way so you will see it constantly. By doing this exercise, you are tapping into motivational superpowers and creating a reminder to *keep going*.

Let's take it one step further.

I like to have a savings account for each goal. If it's truly important to me, I believe a goal deserves a name and a specific place to dwell. I find it doesn't help very much to just have a "Savings Account" and not be specific about what you are saving for. Do you find "savings" motivating? I don't. But if I can give the savings account a name, it conjures up thoughts of the wonderful thing I am saving for, and I find it far more inspiring.

For example, my husband and I love to travel. So we have a "Travel" savings account. Every month we make a deposit into that account. And therein lies the key. We pay into our "Travel" savings like we pay a monthly bill. It's not "when we have some extra money," or it would probably never get done. Instead, it's a part of our monthly budget. We prefer to make room for this, cutting back on other things that aren't as important to us.

What this allows us to do (almost miraculously!) is to take vacations without guilt. Once the "Travel" account has enough money, we get to take a trip. It's that simple. We don't have to figure out where the money is coming from for the trip, because we know it's coming from the Travel savings account.

For us, planning is part of the fun. We set a budget for the trip, estimating the cost of transportation, food, accommodation, adventures, souvenirs, etc. And then it becomes a game. What can we do for free? How can we use airline points? Can we go at a different time of year when prices are lower? Can we stay with friends? Getting creative is part of the adventure.

The payoff also comes after the vacation: if we have spent less money than we had planned (if we have leftover money in the Travel savings account when we get home), then guess what? We get to start planning another trip! For us, that's some juicy motivation.

You can have as many savings accounts as you have goals. There's practically no limit. I currently have eight savings accounts. I honestly can't fund them all at once, but they are there, reminding me of things that are important and motivating me to think of new ways to spend and to save.

This is the way to achieve goals that seem too big and unattainable if you think about trying to fund them all at once. Working goals into your monthly budget is the way that Diane bought her home and the way we are able to go on fun adventures.

Believe it or not, budgeting is the way you can reach the dreams that feel so far away right now, you may not believe you will ever reach them. But reach them, you shall. Because you now have the knowledge and the power to budget wisely, creatively, and effectively. You can do this!

The Peaceful Prosperity Mindset: Expenses

It's okay for money to be fun. I can improve my relationship with money by being creative. I can transform my budget to make money more meaningful in my everyday life.

I choose to make money decisions mindfully with awareness and recognition. I take time to notice how I feel when I am spending money.

I choose a budgeting method that works for me in my current situation. I realize that my situation may change over time, and I can adjust my budget when needed.

I look at money in a holistic way. I know why I spend and why I buy. My choices are aligned with what is most important to me.

I know smart ways to save money. I am excited about trying them out and learning more!

I have savings goals that inspire me. I make saving for my goals a habit. I balance my spending and my saving habits to feel whole and complete.

But wait, there's more!

There's another way to save money and yes, even to make money. This way may surprise you. It's about understanding a weird and wonderful land: the land of CREDIT AND DEBT.

Cue the melodramatic music...

Chapter Four

The Double-Edged Sword: Credit & Debt

"It takes all the running you can do, to keep in the same place. If you want to get somewhere else, you must run at least twice as fast as that!"

—*The Red Queen (Alice Through the Looking Glass)*

In the whimsical books by Lewis Carroll, *Alice's Adventures in Wonderland* and *Alice Through the Looking Glass*, the main character, Alice, falls asleep and wakes up in a fanciful new world where things aren't what they seem. The entire land operates on rules that are quite disconcerting. Up can be down, small can be big, and right can be wrong. Even worse, the land is ruled by the irrational Red Queen, who is eager to chop off the heads of her subjects. Alice does her best to navigate this strange new world and to find her way home while literally keeping her head.

Navigating the world of credit and debt can feel similar. Up can be down, small can be big, and what may seem right may actually be wrong. It can feel overwhelming and disconcerting to try to navigate this land. It can even feel threatening, like you are being hunted by irrational tyrants (not the red queen, perhaps, but credit agencies, debt collectors, etc.). However, if you learn the strange rules of this strange land, you can navigate it. You can even learn to use the rules to your advantage.

So let's jump down the rabbit hole, sort out what this place is all about, and learn how to come out ahead (so to speak... forgive the pun).

First: Where Am I?

Let's start in the land of Credit. In this land, the rulers are the three credit reporting agencies: Equifax, TransUnion, and Experian. Each of them has slightly different preferences, but they all do the same thing: measure specific aspects of your financial behavior and give you a score based on those aspects. A high score is rewarded while a low score may be punished.

So what is "high" and what is "low" when it comes to these scores? Remember we are in a different land, so there's never just one answer to anything.

There are several different methods to calculate your credit score. The most generally accepted is called FICO. Some people use the terms "credit score" and "FICO Score" interchangeably. That's not exactly correct: "credit score" is a generic term (kind of like "facial tissue"). "FICO" is a specific term (kind of like "Kleenex"). (NERD ALERT: FICO originally stood for "Fair, Isaac and Company," after the names of its founders.)

Another scoring method that is becoming popular is called VantageScore. Here's how VantageScore and FICO line up:

Credit score range	VantageScore 3.0	FICO
Excellent	781–850	800–850
Very good	N/A	740–799
Good	661–780	670–739
Fair	601–660	580–669
Poor	500–600	< 580
Very poor	< 500	—

(Source: creditkarma.com)

The three credit reporting agencies tend to lean towards FICO as the standard method for scoring (although sometimes they use a blend). FICO is also what most lenders are looking for, but it depends on the lender. Notwithstanding the chart above, what "good" or "poor" means is also somewhat defined by the person who is looking at your score. The ranges above are not as black and white as they may seem. Also, your score can change from week to week based on the data that flows into the system. Overall, in this land, it is best to think in terms of ranges, rather than getting fixated on precise points.

So how do you know what range you fall into? Thankfully, that part has been made pretty easy for us.

There are many ways to check your score. Many credit card companies and banks offer free credit scores to their customers. You can also go to FICO's website to check your score.

Then there are financial education websites (such as Credit Karma or NerdWallet) that offer you a free score as well as their insights into how you got that score.

If you don't want to use any of these methods, you are entitled to a free credit report every twelve months from each of the three credit reporting agencies. These can be obtained through AnnualCreditReport.com, the official website to do so. (Be wary of other websites that claim to offer free reports and then require you to enter credit card information.) A clever thing to do is to request one report from one agency every four months. Then you can keep an eye on your credit score throughout the year for free!

You should check your credit reports regularly for accuracy, to make sure errors don't pop up and harm your credit score. Checking your credit reports can also alert you to potential identity theft: if you see something you don't recognize on your credit report, investigate it by contacting your lender right away. Often banks and credit card companies will work with you to close fraudulent accounts and, if necessary, alert authorities.

You can dispute errors on your credit report with each of the reporting agencies (Experian, TransUnion, or Equifax). You can also contact the Consumer Financial Protection Bureau (CFPB) if you find anything on your credit report that you didn't authorize. For example, if a company used your information without your permission, you can file a complaint with the CFPB.

You might be thinking, "This doesn't really affect me, Laura. I don't need a new loan or credit card, so why should I care about my credit score?" To which I would say, "Ah my friend, you are still in the Land of Credit, whether you know it or not! Your credit score has tentacles everywhere!"

Your credit score can have a lot of influence on many areas of your financial life, not just how much you can borrow. Having a higher credit score can move you closer to your financial goals by getting you better deals and even discounts. For example...

Just a few things that a high credit score can do for you:

<u>Make your housing options easier and less expensive.</u> When mortgage companies or landlords see a higher credit score, they are more likely to accept you. For a mortgage, a higher score could get you a mortgage at better rates. For a rental, this could mean the difference between getting accepted or getting denied. Both landlords and utility companies can also use your credit score to determine the amount of your security deposit.

<u>Get you a better phone plan.</u> Excellent credit can potentially determine whether a wireless carrier grants you a contract with discounts or a costly month-to-month plan that requires a security deposit.

<u>Earn you a lower interest rate on loans.</u> Potential lenders use your credit score to assess how likely you are to pay back what you borrow. If your score indicates a high likelihood that you will pay back your loan, lenders may offer you better terms to woo you into working with them. This gives you the power to negotiate not only your interest rate but also other elements like a better repayment plan or a higher loan amount.

<u>Lower your car insurance payments.</u> Insurance companies won't turn you away for bad credit, but they may raise rates if they consider you a higher risk. Having a good credit score

indicates you are responsible, which may help to lower your premiums.

Qualify for the best credit cards. The better your credit, the more the credit card companies want you as a customer. They may offer you their juiciest credit card incentives and rewards when you have a high score. You may also qualify for a higher credit limit, which can in turn help boost your credit score.

Help you land a job or promotion. Potential employers must tell you if they will check your credit score when making a hiring decision, but they are permitted to do so. To an employer, a poor credit score could indicate undesirable traits in a prospective employee, like being disorganized, irresponsible, or in financial distress, which could be a red flag for theft or fraud, especially if the job involves handling money. If you are already employed, a high credit score could potentially help you to land a higher security clearance or a promotion.

As you can see, your credit score is not just about loans and interest rates. It follows you into other areas of life, too.

Rick wanted to buy a house with his wife, Carmen. His credit score wasn't high enough to qualify for the mortgage. He told me how he and his wife dreamed of a house where they could raise their three-year-old daughter. "Where we live now is fine," he said with a shrug, "but there's not really a yard for my baby girl to play in, and it can get kind of rowdy at night, which makes for a rough morning the next day. If we could qualify for this house..." his voice trailed off dreamily.

"You could live the life you really want to give your family?" I finished for him.

"Yeah," he agreed.

Rick saw the writing on the wall. Without a better credit score, they were all limited in where and how they could live.

Rick wasn't one to take "no" for an answer. He got serious about improving his credit score.

In addition to making sure he paid his bills on time and paid down his existing debt, he sought out an attorney to help him improve his credit score. The attorney helped him dispute a few items on his report that were inaccurate and negatively affecting his score. Rick also approached his parents about adding his name to their credit card account, which boosted his score immediately.

It took a few months to pay down his debt and dispute the inaccuracies, but doing these things raised his credit score high enough to qualify for a mortgage. In less than a year, he and his family moved into their new house.

But Rick didn't just get into a house through this improvement. His sense of achievement, motivation, and self-confidence also improved.

When I caught up with him, he shared this insight with me. "So you know I improved my credit score and got into a house," he said with a big smile. "But what is really cool is that I find myself making better financial decisions in general. Like, I don't really need that fancy new car now, because I've got a house to pay for. Like, I am proud of paying my house payment because I worked so hard to get it in the first place. I don't want to mess that up again. So I keep finding ways to do better—without anybody telling me I have to. It's weird."

I assured him that was not weird at all.

When you fix one part of your financial life, you taste the victory of improvement. This delicious taste is liberating. When you feel capable of improvement, you liberate yourself from the past. You feel empowered to make better choices that make a positive difference. You can write a new story.

Scavenger Hunt! Find Your Score

Choose one of the sources mentioned above (or another one, if you have a different source you prefer). Find your current credit score and write it down. You can use the worksheet in the *Peaceful Prosperity Workbook* to keep track. Include the date, your score, and the source.

Then, if applicable, write down what you would like your score to be. You could also write down what specific advantages (like those listed above) you want to make a reality in your life. (For example: "I want to improve my credit score to get a better deal on my phone plan.")

In the next few pages, we'll discover how to improve your score. Keep this worksheet handy so you can write down the ideas that you want to act upon.

If you already have great credit, take a moment to reflect upon what that great score has already brought you in your life. How might it continue to contribute to your financial peace and health?

Next: The Weird Rules and How to Play the Game

The Credit Score Game isn't that hard once you know the rules. And once you know the rules, you can become an excellent player. So let's learn the rules.

Five key areas that determine your credit score.

#1: Your Payment History (MOST IMPORTANT).
Paying your bills on time is THE most influential factor
in your credit score.

How to improve here: set up autopay so that you ALWAYS
pay your bills on time, no matter what.

If there's anyone who can tell you about the peace that
autopay can bring to your life, it's Louise. Before she set
up automatic payments, she felt so overwhelmed that she
was having trouble sleeping at night. One night she said to
herself, "I'm an educated woman! This is ridiculous!"

So Louise sat down, got online, and set up automatic
payment for each of her credit cards on the due date each
month.

"This was a big change in my mindset," she noticed. "I had
this little game I used to play where I wouldn't look at the
credit card bill until the last minute. Then I could only pay
what I had left in my bank account at the time—which
was sometimes nothing. It was kind of like I thought, if
I didn't look at it, I could keep spending money on fun
things and wouldn't have to pay the piper. It never worked,
of course."

When I asked her how she made this important change in
mindset, Louise said, "One day I just grew up and decided
this wasn't going to be how it was anymore. I felt embarrassed

and ashamed. That wasn't the way I wanted to be. I thought, I have control over this. I'm going to do something."

Louise didn't blow away her credit card debt overnight. But she changed the tide when she had the bravery to look it in the face and made the decision to change. A few years later, I saw Louise and she told me with a glowing smile that her credit score was up, and her bills were paid on time.

By doing this, Louise did more than improve her credit score. She learned how to budget because she HAD to. After she set up autopay, the credit card bills were going to be paid automatically, whether there was money in her account or not. She couldn't be vague about her money anymore. This trickled into other areas of her life. She discovered that her time management was better because she began to feel responsible and empowered rather than helpless. Her confidence improved as well. As we've been learning, money is never just about money. It affects every area of our lives.

#2: Your credit utilization. (VERY IMPORTANT). To determine this, add up your total credit card balances across all of your cards. Then, add up your credit limits across all of your cards. Divide the balance total by the limits total and you have your credit utilization. (In other words, if you have credit cards but never use them, your utilization could be as low as 0%. If you have credit cards that are "maxed out," your utilization could be as high as 100%.) In this game, the lower score wins.

How to improve here: Aim for a percentage of less than 30%. This can be accomplished by keeping your balances low aka paying off your cards as much as possible. It can also be accomplished by asking your credit card company for a credit limit increase on existing cards. I did this personally several years ago. I had a good payment history, so I was feeling good there. But I thought my score could be higher. When I did the math on credit utilization, I realized that even a small credit increase on a couple of my cards could make a dramatic difference. I timidly called up my credit card companies and guess what? Two out of three of them said yes and gave me a credit limit increase. It wasn't even that much of a big deal or a hassle! My credit score went up and so did my confidence in my financial abilities. Priceless.

#3: The length of your credit history (SOMEWHAT IMPORTANT). This is the amount of time that your credit accounts have been open and when they were last used.

How to improve here: Avoid closing older accounts, and consider using those old cards from time to time. The crucial element here is to use it once, pay it off, and forget about it again. Using credit wisely doesn't mean using all your credit cards all the time. It does mean using them sometimes. Spend and borrow thoughtfully.

#4: Your credit types. (SOMEWHAT IMPORTANT).
It's not just about credit cards. Did you know that there are two types of credit accounts that creditors like to see on your report? There are revolving accounts and there are installment accounts. These two types require slightly different money management and mindset, and lenders like to see that you can master both types.

Revolving credit accounts provide you with flexibility regarding the amount you can charge and pay monthly. These include credit cards, retail store cards, gas cards, and a home equity line of credit (HELOC).

Installment accounts usually start with a fixed balance and then require a fixed payment each month until the balance is paid off. These include mortgages, auto loans, and student loans.

How to improve here: Maintain a healthy mix of both types of accounts. That doesn't mean you should run out and open up new accounts to achieve this. (Read #5 below about the dangers of doing that!) But it does mean that you might begin to think differently about what types of loans and offers you pursue if you are aware of how to keep a healthy credit score.

#5: Your recent credit inquiries (LESS IMPORTANT).
Again, because we are in a strange land, not all credit inquiries will hurt your score.

You may have heard the terms "hard inquiry" and "soft inquiry" and wondered what exactly that meant. Some people mistakenly think that any kind of inquiry is detrimental to your credit score. If that is you, I have good news! That's not the case.

Hard inquiries are when you've given someone permission to check your credit report to process a credit or loan application. This only happens when you apply for a loan or a refinance.

Soft inquiries don't require your approval and can happen anytime. They can happen when you check your credit score or when an employer does a background check on you. Ever receive a "pre-approved" offer from a lender? That means a "soft inquiry" was done before they contacted you. They checked you out first to see if they wanted to make you an offer. But it doesn't affect your score.

Only hard inquiries have any effect, and the effect tends to wear off after a few months. A hard inquiry does, however, stay on your credit report for two years.

How to improve here: Avoid unnecessary hard inquiries. This includes those tempting store credit cards at the time of checkout. You know, the ones that tempt you with: "Would you like to open up a (insert store name here) credit card and save 10% today? It's easy and fast and you'll receive more money-saving offers throughout the year as a cardholder!"

When the cashier purrs these familiar words to you, I want you to picture the Cheshire Cat leering down at you with a mischievous smile. This could be a trap. Before you say yes, think about three things:

Am I currently seeking any other loans or credit, or will I be soon? Opening multiple accounts in a short period can be a red flag to lenders and may result in denials or higher rates. Bad.

How much will this actually save me today? 10% on a $50.00 purchase is a whopping $5.00. Is it worth saving $5.00 to put a hard inquiry on your credit report that will sit there for two years?

How often will I use the benefits of this card? Let's say you do open it. Will you use the "money-saving offers" in the future? Will you be tempted to use the card to purchase more than you would otherwise? (That's what the store is betting on... which is why that cat has such a mischievous grin.)

I'm not saying store cards are always a bad idea. I am saying don't let the riddles of the charming Cheshire Cat befuddle you into signing up for something you don't need.

PRO TIP: Equifax recommends holding two to three credit cards in addition to other types of credit (like a mortgage) to get or maintain a good credit score. Experian reports that the average American has around four credit cards. There is no maximum that you are allowed to have so it's up to you to keep track. The key is knowing your capacity and managing your debt. Don't get in over your head or you may lose it!

Scavenger Hunt, Continued! Improve Your Score

Now that you know ways you can improve your credit score, go back to the Credit Worksheet and write down one to two ideas you will implement this week. You might even schedule them into your calendar like this: "On Tuesday, I will call Citibank and ask them about a credit line increase."

Then, find a date six months from now. Make a note in your calendar to check your credit score again on that date. Write it down on the sheet. Hopefully, you will see your progress! This is a powerful motivator. It's like seeing "before" and "after" photos of your newly renovated bathroom. It can make you feel really good.

Don't Lose Your Head: Other Credit Games

Credit cards can have other advantages, too. Yep, I am talking about REWARDS!! Cue the fireworks and ticker tape parade!!

...and more weird rules. Of course.

Rewards programs can be mind-boggling when it comes to trying to maximize and strategize how you spend and how you claim your rewards. What works for one person may be a disaster for someone else. Even when you do find your "bestie" rewards card, you may occasionally be surprised by rewards caps or blackout dates that you weren't aware of until you try using your rewards. What's a smart shopper to do?

First, know that the internet is your friend. There are websites galore that will help you to do the analysis and crunch the numbers on different rewards programs.

Some websites will compare the cash value of rewards. Some websites will recommend cards to you based on your spending habits and goals! (Bankrate.com, Nerdwallet.com, and thepointsguy.com are a few I have explored.) Take a stroll around cyberspace and see what you can find.

Next, to help with the potential overwhelm in this rabbit hole, consider these three reflection questions when reviewing rewards programs. You can use these for current cards you hold or new cards you might consider. Taking a moment to think about these three areas can set you up for a better credit card experience.

What kinds of rewards are the most appealing to me? Which rewards will I actually use?

The three most common types of rewards are cash back, points, and mile-earning cards. When my husband and I looked at these, we noticed that miles-earning cards were the most appealing to us because we like to travel. We know we are going to travel anyway, so why not have a rewards card that would reward us for something we already do? For us, a miles-earning card also allows us to travel more inexpensively. When we earn enough miles, we can fly for free. And if we are staying at home, we can use our miles to purchase flights for others to come see us!

However, a miles-earning card wouldn't be at all interesting to someone like my aunt who doesn't like to travel. So you need to know what you want and what you will use before signing up for the card.

Also, be aware of caps and limitations on using your wonderful rewards. For my husband and I, we need to be on the lookout for blackout dates when we can't use our miles to purchase our airfare—or when the price of using miles is higher than the price of just purchasing a ticket outright. We also need to make sure we are using our miles regularly because miles can expire if unused. What a bummer that would be if we weren't able to use the benefits after all that due diligence to earn them!

What do I spend the most money on and how much effort do I want to put into maximizing rewards?

If you spend a lot in one budget category, it could make sense to find a rewards program that rewards that specific kind of spending. For example, if you drive often, a gas rewards program could be a great idea for you. If you have a pretty big grocery bill each month, you could seek a card that offers bonuses for purchases at grocery stores. (I once heard of a card that offered 6% cash back on grocery purchases but only 1% on other types of purchases.)

I have a friend who keeps extensive spreadsheets on the bonus "shopping categories" for each of his cards each month. He changes out the card in his wallet depending on what the category is. For example, if one of his cards offers a 5% bonus for purchases made at a gas station, he'll make sure to use that card when he fills his tank... this month. Next month it will probably change. He's a clever guy and frankly, it's a fun game for him. It doesn't sound like much fun to me. I know that I seek a lower-effort rewards system. To each his own.

What are the fees?

Credit cards that offer rewards usually have some kind of annual fee. Even if you like the rewards program, and even if "all fees are waived the first year," be sure to check out what the annual fee is. If the annual fee is more than what you are saving by using the rewards, you could be as topsy-turvy as the Mad Hatter. This also brings up another good practice: evaluate your spending and rewards cards from time to time (perhaps annually or when life changes for you). You can always change rewards programs to adjust to changes in your life. For example, if my husband and I ever get burned out on travel, we might change to a cash-back rewards program. Or ditch the rewards cards altogether and opt for a simple no-fee credit card. It all depends on your personal preferences.

Another note: if you carry a balance on your card, then rewards cards might not be the way to go at all. Rewards cards can have higher interest rates than other cards, so they may only be worthwhile if you can pay off your balance most months.

Myths About Credit

Myth #1: "I've messed up and it will haunt me forever! I'M DOOMED!"

Don't believe this voice if you hear it inside your head. You can always improve your situation, no matter how dire it may feel.

First, know that negative credit information typically "ages off" or falls off your report over time. As we learned earlier, a "hard inquiry" takes two years to fall off your report. More serious items typically stick around for seven years (this includes late payments, foreclosures, collections, and money owed to the government). The longest negative item, bankruptcy, stays on your report for ten years. I'm not saying that bankruptcy is not very serious. I am saying that as challenging as that situation is, even bankruptcy doesn't stick around on your credit report until doomsday. Thankfully, it seems even credit reporting agencies realize that we learn, change, and grow over time.

"It's no use going back to yesterday, because I was a different person then."

—*The Caterpillar (Alice's Adventures in Wonderland)*

Other useful things to know: medical debt that is owed directly to medical providers is treated slightly differently from other types of debt. Several years ago, credit reporting agencies agreed to soften the rules on this type of debt. Medical debt may not factor as heavily into your credit score as other accounts in collection. Some of the agencies even ignore medical collection accounts that are less than six months old.

The credit agencies made this change to allow consumers time to resolve disputes with medical providers or insurance companies or develop a payment plan. (Please note: this is only for a debt owed directly to a doctor, hospital, or lab. If you paid medical expenses using a credit card, it is viewed as credit card debt, not medical debt.)

If you have medical debt, take advantage of this! Start talking to your providers and work out a payment plan. Not only can you potentially save money, but you can also potentially save yourself other headaches by keeping your credit report healthy.

<u>Myth #2:</u> "Do not open credit cards. Pay cash for everything. All debt is EVIL AND BAD!"

By now, I am hoping you have learned some examples of how credit can help you with your financial goals. A good credit score can get you better deals in a variety of ways, affecting not only your finances but also your daily life and well-being. And a good credit score comes from having and managing debt.

Debt managed responsibly can help you build leverage, which is another magical tool in this strange land! Let's peek into the last weird and wonderful concept that makes many people feel upside-down.

"There is good debt and bad debt. It is wise to pay off bad debt – or not get into it in the first place. Simply said, bad debt takes money out of your pocket, and good debt puts money into your pocket." —Robert Kiyosaki

Robert Kiyosaki, author of the book *Rich Dad, Poor Dad* (among others), is famous for observing that wealthy people tend to think differently about money from people who are poor. One of the key differences he likes to comment upon is how successful people think about credit and debt. Wealthy people tend to view debt as leverage, creating potential opportunities and advantages.

One of the easiest ways to visualize how leverage works is to think of a mortgage. A young family starting out probably does not have hundreds of thousands of dollars to purchase a home with cash, so they apply for a mortgage. This type of debt allows them to purchase a house when they otherwise could not have done so. That's what leverage can do for you. It can help you reach your financial goals faster than you could have otherwise.

Pam understands leverage. When she was in her 40s, she decided to take out a Home Equity Line of Credit (HELOC) on her existing home. This is different from a mortgage. A

HELOC allows you to access the equity in your home and turn it into cash you can use. Pam's house was not paid off, but she had owned it for many years. She had built up a good amount of equity by making regular mortgage payments. Also, the real estate market in her local area was doing well, which increased the value of her home even more.

Realizing this could be a resource that she could tap into, Pam worked with her bank to open up a HELOC. Usually this involves an application and review process, like opening a credit card. After Pam was approved and had access to new cash, how she used that cash is a great example of leverage.

Pam put a down payment on another house. This meant taking out another mortgage, which could have been frightening, but Pam had a plan. She rented out the second home, rather than living in it. She calculated the rent payments so they were fair for the area, but enough to cover the second mortgage. She made sure the rent payments would also be enough to cover the taxes, insurance, utilities, and repairs on the property. Here's what that meant for Pam: now, instead of owning one home, she owned two, but someone else (her renter) was paying for the second home! That, my friends, is leverage. It is a key to building wealth.

Just like credit, leverage comes with its own rules and dangers, as well as its advantages. Learning how to use it can be its own rabbit hole, so let's leave that for another day. For now,

I simply want to point out this rabbit hole to you as another place to explore. It is another world that can be accessed with an open mind.

"The Queen turned crimson with fury, and, after glaring at her for a moment like a wild beast, began screaming, "Off with her head! Off with..."

"Nonsense!" said Alice, very loudly and decidedly, and the Queen was silent."

—Alice's Adventures in Wonderland

Now that you know the rules of the land of credit and you know how to play the game, you should feel your confidence growing. Like Alice, you can speak up with conviction, armed with the knowledge of where you stand, how this land operates, and what you can do to make the most of it.

Now that we have our heads about us, this is the perfect position from which to tackle the next topic: debt. I know without a doubt that you will be able to silence this enemy as well.

DEBT

Gene looked back at me through her dark eyes hidden behind thick dark glasses. She swallowed repeatedly before speaking. Her mouth was very dry.

"It's like... I have this recurring dream," she said. "I'm walking along this path near the beach. I'm totally fine, it's a beautiful day. And then, before I even know it, I am sinking into quicksand! I try to get out, and I can't move. The pressure around me makes it hard to breathe. I can't cry out for help but there isn't any anyway and I know I am going to suffocate."

"What happens next?" I asked.

"I wake up," she said simply. "And hope it never happens again."

This vivid image was Gene's reply when I asked her to describe how debt feels. Can you relate to her description? Does debt feel like quicksand to you? Maybe to you, debt feels like a heavy ball and chain around your ankle that holds you back. Maybe it feels like a bad grade on a report card that means you'll get a reprimand. Or maybe it feels like a shadowy ghost, something otherworldly, mysterious, and possibly threatening.

Whatever debt feels like to you, I want you to take a moment to explore this. It doesn't matter whether you have a lot of debt, zero debt, or somewhere in between. Let's take a moment now to consider what debt means to you.

Listen to Your Words

Try this. Write down all the words, images, and sensations that come to your mind when you hear the word DEBT. (You can use the Debt Worksheet in the *Peaceful Prosperity Workbook* if you like.) Take as long as you wish, but you should probably have enough after just a few minutes.

Now, take a step back and gain some distance from these words. As much as possible, without judging, simply observe what those words and images are. Perhaps you can picture yourself far away from those words and images, a distant observer. What can you observe from a distance? Take a moment to write down your observations.

I want you to know that words matter! Unexamined words can feel like enemies. Deliberately chosen words can be powerful allies.

For example, notice the difference between:

"I'm broke" and "I'm not making as much money as I would like."

"I've failed" and "I have the opportunity to try again more intelligently."

"I should have done that differently..." and "I could have done that differently..."

"I have to do this..." and "I want to do this..."

Words not only affect your self-esteem and your attitude, they also influence your actions. By changing the words that you use when you are faced with debt, you can change the course of your life.

The subtle shift in how you approach debt can mean the difference between doing nothing and having your situation get worse, or feeling empowered to act and improving your situation.

"Talk as if you're a powerful person, not a victim... Life follows what you say... What you focus on expands. It's never the other way around."

—Barbara Stanny

Go back to the words you have written down regarding DEBT. What subtle shifts can you make to your language, to change the way debt feels to you?

In *Harry Potter and the Prisoner of Azkaban,* there is a wonderful scene where Professor Lupin teaches his students a spell called "RIDDIKULUS!" He asks each student to come to the front of the class and imagine something that is terrifying to them. As the scary image appears in front of each student, they practice the spell by shouting out "RIDDIKULUS!" and thinking of something funny instead. This causes the frightening thing in front of them to turn into something laughable.

A menacing snake turns into a goofy clown. A giant spider suddenly wears roller skates, slips, and falls. When you can laugh, fear goes flying out the window. The key, says Professor Lupin, is using your imagination very clearly and confidently. You can do that, too.

This is how you begin to "wake up" from the "bad dream" of debt.

The answer is not in replaying how you got there or beating yourself up about the past. The answer is in standing in front of the thing that scares you and using your mind – the power of your imagination – to change it into something you can handle, even laugh at.

BONUS CHALLENGE: Can you give your debt a persona? Is it an animal or a person? What does it look like, sound like, and smell like?

Next, can you imagine something ridiculous, as the students in the Harry Potter story did? Can you overlay that ridiculous image on top of your debt image?

For example, let's say your debt image is a huge, hairy wolf howling at your door. Can you picture throwing him a hot pink chew toy that makes a silly noise? And then imagine that the frightening wolf shrinks down to a puppy who gives up howling and starts licking the toy with glee!

This might seem silly, but this exercise has the potential to give you surprising power.

You can journal in the *Peaceful Prosperity Workbook* about your thoughts here and other images you can use to build a sense that you have control and power over your debt, rather than it having control and power over you.

SHRINKING AND GROWING

We've already hinted at the idea that not all debt is the same. Some debt is considered "good" while some debt is considered "bad." Let's take that a bit further.

First, let's define two kinds of debt.

Meet Secured Debt. This type of debt is backed by a tangible thing, aka "collateral." Common examples of secured debt are an auto loan, where the collateral is your car; or a mortgage, where the collateral is your house.

Because there is some tangible assurance that the loan will be repaid, lenders (banks) tend to like this type of loan. When you think about the word, it makes sense: lenders feel relatively *secure* that the debt will be repaid. If it is not, they can take back the collateral, and at least they have something in their hands.

Secured debt means less risk to the lender, so the terms are often more favorable to the borrower (you). If you have a good credit score, lenders might even compete for your business! Overall, secured debt potentially means lower interest rates and higher loan amounts. For these reasons, some people would say this is "good debt."

Meet Unsecured Debt. This type of debt requires no "security" or physical object to back it up. Repaying it is simply a promise. Common examples are credit cards or student loans.

As you can imagine, this kind of debt is riskier for lenders. They must base the terms on the creditworthiness of the borrower (i.e., your credit score), rather than on the value of the underlying collateral. There's not much else to go on.

This means that unsecured debt usually gets hit with higher interest rates, shorter payment terms, and lower loan amounts. For these reasons, some people would say this is "bad debt."

"Good" and "bad" can be subjective, though. It is possibly more helpful to think of each kind of debt as having different effects on your financial life. To illustrate this—please bear with me—I'm going to go back to a scene in *Alice in Wonderland*.

At one point in the story, Alice discovers a bottle of liquid that says "Drink Me." After pondering whether or not the contents might be poison, Alice decides to drink the liquid. She discovers that it tastes delicious! It also allows her to shrink so that she can go through a tiny door to a beautiful garden that she had been admiring. Alice's short-term wish has been granted. But, as you can imagine, being tiny has its difficulties.

Next, Alice finds a cake marked "Eat Me." When she does so, she becomes tall again, not only back to her normal height, but even beyond that, to the size of a giant! This, too, brings problems, but you can see how the effect is very different. Each experience allows Alice to accomplish different results.

Unsecured debt can have the effect of "drink me" – quick, easy, and useful in the short term. There's nothing wrong with that. The key is using it for the short term. If you can manage to pay off the unsecured debt in the short term, you can use it as a helpful tool. But in the long term, it can cause you to shrink financially.

Secured debt, on the other hand, can have the effect of "eat me" – being the catalyst for you to reach new heights (like owning a home or two, as Pam did!). It must be handled and managed just as carefully and responsibly as unsecured debt, but if handled with knowledge and respect, it can help you to grow.

"Would you tell me, please, which way I ought to go from here?"

"That depends a good deal on where you want to get to," said the Cat.

"I don't much care where..." said Alice.

"Then it doesn't matter which way you go," said the Cat.

—Alice's Adventures in Wonderland

Now that you have gotten to know the characteristics of debt, where do you go from here? Well, that depends on what you want to do. Most people want to get rid of their debt, especially the unsecured kind. Let's do that.

There's a simple acronym I like to use to help remember three simple steps to get out of debt: W.I.N.

W.I.N. the Debt Game

You've already begun winning the debt game (did you know that?)! Possibly the most important piece to controlling your debt is to work on your budget. If you're this far, you know the importance of building your income and managing your expenses, and you've already got a powerful toolkit to help you do that.

Now you can go even further. Let's WIN!

W = Write it all down

You've been very brave looking the debt beast in the eye. Now let's see what he's made of. We're going to write down all of your debts. If you start to feel overwhelmed, you can use the Debt Worksheet in the *Peaceful Prosperity Workbook* and let it guide you. Write down the kind of debt (Creditor), how much it is (Balance), what the interest rate is (Rate), and what the monthly minimum payment is (Payment). NOTE: The "payment" in this exercise is NOT how much you pay monthly. Rather, it is the minimum amount the lender requires you to pay.

After you have done this, you know exactly what you are dealing with. Talk about power! Let's look at some different ways to tackle your debt.

The first method, made hugely popular by Dave Ramsey, is called the "Debt Snowball" method. You pay off the debts with the *smallest balance first*, working your way up to the largest balance. Since your total monthly debt payment always stays the same, even as you pay off smaller debts, that means by the time you get to focusing on your largest debt, you are putting a lot of money towards paying it off. That's why it's referred to as a "snowball" —you keep rolling payments forward like you roll a snowball on the ground to make it bigger and bigger. By the time you are done, you have a pretty large, powerful weapon in your hands that can beat down debt quickly.

A slightly different method is called the "Debt Avalanche" method. This is the more "math-y" way to approach debt. The Avalanche prioritizes debts that carry a high-interest rate, regardless of the balance. In other words, you pay off the *most expensive debt first,* and work down to the least expensive. Usually, this results in a lower amount of total interest paid over time. However, I find it particularly interesting to compare how much of a difference this makes. Sometimes, depending on your debts, the difference between the Snowball method and the Avalanche method is not that large.

Finally, you can customize the priority of your debts in some other fashion. For example, let's say you have a credit card with a balance and an interest rate that would normally cause it to fall somewhere in the middle of the Snowball or Avalanche methods. But you know that on this cards, there is a 0% interest special deal which expires in eighteen months. YTo take advantage of this special deal, you can make paying off that card your first priority with a timeline of less than eighteen months. Then you can switch to another method.

I = Implement a plan

Ultimately, it doesn't matter which method you choose. What matters is that you DO it. Choose a method, create a plan, and stick to it.

I know. "Easier said than done, Laura!" Here are a few "brain hacks" that clients have used to stick to their debt payoff plans.

Heather printed out her debt payoff schedule and stuck it to her refrigerator. Each month, when she made her payments, she checked off another box and watched her progress. She could see the finish line and how close she was to it. This motivated her to keep going, even when the going got tough some months. Heather paid off her $11,000 credit card debt in less than 2 years.

Visual scoreboards can be powerful motivators. Ever notice how charities will often post a running goal board during a fundraiser? Donors can see the progress and know they are making a difference. The goal board can also spur a flurry of additional last-minute donations when donors see how just a few extra dollars will get the organization across the finish line to reach the goal! The same can be true for paying off debt.

We like the sense of satisfaction we get when we cross a finish line. Grant yourself this motivator and visualize this joy. When a debt is paid off and your goal is reached, let the (real or imaginary) crowd CHEER! It's important that you celebrate your victories.

Juanita used a similar idea but with individual Post-it notes. Once she made up her mind and had her debt payoff plan, she wrote down affirmations on a variety of colored Post-it notes. She used general ones like "I've got this!" to very specific ones like "I will be debt free by December!" She posted the affirmations all over her house where she would run into them: on her bathroom mirror, in her pantry, by her shoes, inside her cabinet, and in her wallet! These small reminders delighted her as she went through her day, like small allies cheering her on to her goal. Juanita paid off her remaining car debt in 7 months.

Yvonne made her debt payoff into a friendly competition with her brother. Growing up, they had always been competitive, so it occurred to her that they could use this as a motivator for both of them to do better in their financial lives. Yvonne told her brother that she was confident she could pay off her debt faster than he could pay off his. Game on!

Each of them reported to the other monthly. It started off just telling each other how much money they had put towards their debts, seeing who could pay down the most. But then it got better. After Yvonne had paid off her credit cards, she challenged her brother to a mortgage payoff smack-down. They got so creative in finding small ways to save money to put towards their mortgages that they BOTH paid off their homes several years before they expected to! How's that for sibling rivalry?

Yvonne had experienced the power of the last letter in WIN = using her Network.

N = Network to build support and keep going!

Having a friend or relative as your "accountability buddy" can be a helpful tool to successfully pay off debt—or reach any financial goal—as Yvonne discovered with her brother. Just like having a "gym buddy" who gets up and meets you for a workout is more likely to make you go to that workout (even when you don't feel like it), so, too, can a financial accountability partner help to motivate you and keep you on track to your financial goals. This person could be a spouse, a trusted friend, or even a professional money coach. Go with whomever makes you feel most motivated and inspired.

Most importantly, you should know that you don't have to do this alone.

Who's in your network? Take a moment now to list five potential people you can reach out to for support in achieving your financial goals. These could be friends, family, or co-workers. Think about what inspires you about each person. How you would like to engage with them? What the potential benefits are for each of you? Brainstorming this ahead of time can build your courage, if needed, in asking these helpers to join you in pursuit of your goal. Maybe they have something they want to achieve, as well. Remember that by working together, you can both W.I.N.!

Special Considerations

This section on Credit and Debt is not meant to be exhaustive. That would require its own book entirely! Rather, I intend to encourage you to look at credit and debt in new ways and to give you the language to discover even more information on your own.

Other topics you may want to consider and research, depending on your particular situation, include:

- How the debt of others in your life can affect YOU. This can come in two flavors:

  - your responsibility for your partner's debt, especially in community property states. Be sure to get clear on what is "yours, mine, and ours" now. Becoming familiar with this will help you make better decisions both now and in the event of divorce or death of either partner.

  - your responsibility when you help others by adding their name to your credit card OR being a co-signer on a loan. This can be a great boost to a loved one (like a child) *or* it can be a huge financial burden that can ruin a relationship.

- Declaring bankruptcy: this is not to be taken lightly, but it is an option. Know the pros and cons, the implications, and what you might consider before making this huge financial decision.

- When you might want to reach out for professional help. An accountant, attorney, financial planner, or debt consolidation expert might be well worth your time, money, and effort in some cases. Don't rule them out. If you are feeling overwhelmed or at a dead end, talking to a professional can help move you toward a solution that you might not be able to see on your own.

Here are examples of a few of the people and organizations that can help:

- Getting a handle on your debt:

  - https://debtorsanonymous.org/

  - https://financialrecovery.com/

- Debt consolidation resources:

  - https://www.greenpath.com

  - https://credit.org/cccs/

  - https://www.freedomdebtrelief.com/

- Financial Therapists:

  - https://www.financialtherapyassociation.org/

"Well, now that we have seen each other," said the Unicorn, "if you'll believe in me, I'll believe in you. Is that a bargain?"

—Alice's Adventures in Wonderland

Wow! You've read about some complex financial concepts in this chapter. Some of the exercises have required a lot of work, thought, and research. If you'd like to pause for a moment and do a meditation, you certainly have earned it! There is a guided meditation in the *Peaceful Prosperity Workbook* to help you relax and integrate all the information you have gone through so far. Be sure to take a breath and like Alice, give yourself a moment to acknowledge you've been through quite an adventure!

The Peaceful Prosperity Mindset: Credit & Debt

My mind is sharp, clear, and alert. I will not be confused by jargon and weird rules. I know how to play the credit game.

I know my credit score, what it means, and how it impacts my life.

I have the courage to face my debt and know that it is a temporary situation. I have a plan to get out of debt and the confidence that I can do this.

I believe that living with credit and debt is part of my financial journey. I release any shame I may feel about my credit score or having debt.

I am open to the idea that not all debt is bad. I see that debt can be also used as a tool to create leverage and help me on my financial journey.

I am empowered to improve my financial situation. I surround myself with people who help me to support my financial goals.

CONGRATULATIONS ON COMPLETING YOUR ASCENT: BUILDING MINDFUL BUDGETS

How are you doing, my friend?

In climbing up the mountain in the first section, you may have shaken off some old beliefs and left them behind you. You may be considering new attitudes. You may have changed some old habits, or you may be working on some new ones. You have already come a long way from where you started. You are climbing up your financial mountain.

You may now be slightly surprised that you have more in your toolbox than you thought you did when you first started on this trek. Let's take a look back and appreciate what we have covered so far:

You know mindset and methods to have a better relationship with money.

You know your current income sources and how you can expand them.

You know your expense categories and have chosen more meaningful ways to interact with them.

You know the crazy language of the Land of Credit and how to play the game.

I hope you can hear me applauding.

You probably don't know it, but you are now sitting on the top of the mountain which we have set out to climb. That does not mean we are done with the journey. We still have landscapes to explore ahead of us. But here, at the top of the mountain, is where we can take a deep breath, celebrate, and EXPAND. Up here, we can see with an entirely new perspective—the result of our work so far—and this new perspective can change everything.

"The best view comes after the hardest climb."

—Anonymous

I am so excited for you to see the next section. You are ready!

THE SUMMIT: EXPANDING YOUR VISION

"Vision is a destination – a fixed point to which we focus all effort. Strategy is a route – an adaptable path to get us where we want to go."

—Simon Sinek

Chapter Five: Balance Sheet Discoveries

Chapter Six: Money Dates and Money Conversations

Have you ever taken a moment to envision what you really want out of life?

I'm not talking about "wishing" or "daydreaming" (though those can be useful, too!). The kind of envisioning I am talking about is a bit like meditation. It's about tapping in to something you feel or sense, but may not have had the opportunity to fully express.

A friend once compared envisioning to "writing a journal entry describing something that hasn't happened just yet." In envisioning her ideal life, she wrote about it as if she were living it now, rather than in the future. This helped her make her ideal life vision more concrete and real. You may have heard that our brains can't differentiate between reality and a strong vision. Let's use this technique to "trick" your brain into moving toward your ideal life and making it a reality.

Writing a "future" journal entry is one way to expand your thinking. You can write freeform, describing the events of your day, your feelings and what inspires you. Or, in the *Peaceful Prosperity Workbook*, there's an "Ideal Life Exercise" to help you envision your ideal life in detail.

If words are difficult to find, you can use pictures that represent your idel life. These can be pictures you cut out from magazines or digital pictures you save in an "Ideal Life" folder. Better yet, you can compile photos in a collage or

"Vision Board" (physical or digital) and keep this in a place where you will see it often.

Whether you create a journal entry or a vision board – or both! – refer back to your Ideal Life Vision often in this next section.

To paraphrase Simon Sinek, your vision will serve as your "fixed point" as we move into some strategies to get you to where you want to go.

Now, take a breath of the clean, crisp mountain air. Enjoy the freshness of your new perspective. In this section, we will widen our view, refine our skills, and feel the freedom to reimagine.

Chapter Five
Balance Sheet Discoveries

"Over every mountain, there is a pass, although it may not be seen from the valley."

—*Theodore Roethke*

I'd like to ask you to try something. Can you stand on one foot? What do you feel? Go ahead – give it a try. (Unless you're riding the subway or something. Then you may want to just pretend). You might feel a little wobbly or unstable. Or you might feel just fine. Now try standing on the other foot. What's that like? Often your two sides feel quite different. That's normal.

Now stand on both feet and take a deep breath. Chances are, it's easier for you to maintain your balance when you are standing on both feet.

This little exploration shows us the importance of having a balance sheet. (Oh, you can sit down now. Thanks.) There are two sides, which you must balance out, to feel financially stable. If you feel like you're financially unstable, it could be because you've got a lopsided balance sheet.

What's a Balance Sheet?

The two sides of a balance sheet are assets and liabilities. Simply put, an asset is something that you OWN. Some examples are: your house; a savings account; a retirement account; stocks, bonds, or other investments.

A liability is something that you OWE. Some examples are: a car loan; credit cards; a mortgage or Home Equity Line of Credit (HELOC); or a student loan.

So a balance sheet is a list of all of that STUFF (assets and liabilities), with a simple calculation at the end: Assets minus Liabilities. I like to say this is the baseline for your financial health. But it's more than just that. Your balance sheet is also your gateway to discovery.

"We'll find it in the balance sheet," said April. She and her husband, Josh, were just finishing up an annual review with me, their financial advisor. I like to end these meetings on a forward-thinking high note, talking about the goals and priorities for the next 12 months. April and Josh had just purchased a home in Colorado. They were looking forward to giving it some updates. In addition to new paint and countertops, they were thinking about solar panels and a hot tub. It was just a matter of figuring out where the money would come from to fund these projects. That's where April's comment about "finding it in the balance sheet" came in.

I've never seen anyone rock a balance sheet like April and Josh. When they first got married, they talked about their dreams, as so many newlyweds do. (And should!) Then, they took their dreams a step further to bring them into reality. How? They used a balance sheet.

It may sound odd, but by building a balance sheet together, they built a better relationship. Not only did they get a handle on their numbers, but they also gained a sense of trust and intimacy by sharing their financial details. Then they could problem-solve together. They played to each other's strengths by listening openly to the observations and suggestions of the other. Finally, they had an open discussion and came up with compromises they could both agree upon.

For example, they each had student loan debt they weren't thrilled about. They could see it on their balance sheet. So the first year, they decided to focus on paying off their student loans. The next year, they decided to focus on investing and retirement. They didn't pay off their student loans in one year, by the way, but they made enough progress that they felt comfortable changing their focus in year two. This is how they could stay balanced. Each year they would reassess their focus, agreeing upon that year's plan. And knowing that their plans would grow and change as their lives unfolded.

According to April and Josh, each year, it just got better. Now they are in their 12th year of marriage and have achieved more goals than they ever thought possible – because they work together on their balance sheet.

"We're such nerds!" April confessed. "Once, during a winter storm, we were holed up in the house for a few days. We got bored. We decided to go over our numbers. We actually projected our balance sheet onto our empty wall like a movie! We worked on a few things, I don't remember exactly what, but I'm embarrassed to say, we had so much fun!" Working with their balance sheet is how they were able to set their financial priorities – and how you can, too.

Let's be clear: I used to hate balance sheets. Ryan would squeal with delight at the idea of sitting down annually and making all "our numbers" line up in neat columns. Meanwhile, I would try to conceal my massive eye-roll. Really? It felt self-aggrandizing to write down all the stuff we owned, and even worse, it felt deflating to write down all the stuff we owed. WHY do this at all? If we mastered our budget, kept our heads down, and paid off debt as much as we could, wasn't that good enough? Wasn't that the secret to getting ahead? Well, yes and no. The budget is where it all *starts*, but it's not where it all *ends!* To truly get ahead, you need a balance sheet.

It's your balance sheet, not your budget, that shows you the long-term effects of your day-to-day financial behavior. In other words, as you go through your daily life, spending and saving, the cumulation of these actions appears in your balance sheet.

Stopping at your budget is short-term thinking. It's like planting seeds in a garden and then walking away before the harvest. Don't do that! If you plant your seeds with intention, you can better enjoy your harvest! Your balance sheet gives purpose to your budget. It also expands your thinking, lighting the way for where to go next.

On the day that I finally "got" this, the power of the balance sheet suddenly jumped off the page and hit me in the face! If you've ever seen the movie "Wizard of Oz," you know that moment when the movie changes from black and white to color? That's what this felt like for me.

Ever since then, I LOVE doing our annual balance sheet. Ryan and I take time every New Year's Day (when, honestly, not much else is going on) and cozy up in our home office to work through our numbers. We talk about where we were this time last year. We laugh over fond memories and cry over sorrowful ones. We talk about where we want to be in one, three, or five years. We envision what we'll do with friends, family, and our time on Earth. We talk about what impact we would like to make in our communities, our industry, and the world.

Wait, WHAT? You can get all this good, juicy stuff out of a balance sheet conversation? YES! Read on.

HOW TO CREATE A PEACEFUL & PROSPEROUS BALANCE SHEET

<u>Step 1.</u>

Bring out your Balance Sheet. If you don't have one, there is a great starter template in the *Peaceful Prosperity Workbook*, or you can create your own in a program like Excel. This is where you get organized. Once you create a good template, you'll just copy it to a new tab and update it each year, so it gets easier the more you do it.

Step 2.

Dig up your accounts! This can be the overwhelming part, so breathe and take it one step at a time. You probably know how to log in to your checking account. Do that. Find your balance as of today's date. Don't worry about all the ins and outs, or about the fact that it will likely change tomorrow, or that it's not absolutely perfect! (ARRRRGGG!) It's okay. This isn't meant to be perfect. It's meant to be a snapshot, a sketch, a work in progress; not a masterpiece painting that is worthy of being hung up in a museum forever.

Step 3.

Fill in the template. Account by account. One by one. You may find some accounts you had forgotten about. Add them. You may forget about some accounts and have to go back and fill them in later. It's okay and it's all part of the process. The only rule is that you need to find the actual account balance as of today's date. Rounding it off is ok, but no guessing. Look it up. Persistence pays off here! Just imagine how great it will feel to have it all filled in accurately. You can do this!

Here's another idea, if you're willing to try it. For us, this is a great "couples" task. I realize this may not be true for everyone, but it is for us. We have A LOT of accounts. Gathering all the data could be a pain for one person, so we break it up. I look up my accounts, and Ryan looks up his. I look up the insurance info, and Ryan looks up the investments. Etcetera. It's kind of like breaking up household chores: you dust, I'll vacuum. And then we get the whole house cleaner, faster, together. We also both feel like we have a stake and a say in the outcome (whether that is the cleanliness of the house or the completion of the balance sheet).

Step 4.

Step back and TAKE A BREAK. Seriously. Walk around. Eat something. (Ryan and I are usually doing this on New Year's Day, so an occasional beverage break or snack break is entirely appropriate.) Working with the Balance Sheet is not a quick exercise. It can take a couple of hours. You need to take time to digest it all.

Step 5.

Now, come back and observe. What do you see? What sticks out to you right away? There's usually something. Maybe it's that student loan debt you hate to look at. Maybe the balance in your IRA is more or less than you had thought. Maybe your car loan is close to being paid off. This is exactly the kind of insight the balance sheet offers that the budget cannot. Here's where your world goes from black and white to technicolor! (If you need help knowing where to look, there's a series of questions in the *Peaceful Prosperity Workbook*.)

With this new insight, you can examine whatever it was that stuck out to you. Ask yourself, "Now why is that? Why does that matter to me? What is at stake here?"

Next, get curious. Ask: "Do I need to do anything? If so, what?"

This is where the balance sheet and the budget begin to work together and you can make real progress.

Let's take the example of that student loan. You hate seeing that on there, so you wonder how you can get rid of it. Let's go to your budget and take a look. How can you direct more money to paying off that student loan?

Maybe you can cancel a gym membership or a streaming service you never use. Or maybe you decide to start packing your lunch instead of eating out. Or maybe you heard about a refinance offer and you decide to check that out. See? All the wheels are turning!

Step 6.

Write down your observations and the questions you have. Then, write down the one next step you need to do. If it motivates you, you might also write down a due date. For example, "I notice that I get a sinking feeling in my stomach when I look at the balance of my student loan. What can I do to pay it off faster. Call the loan company when I have lunch on Tuesday. Are there other repayment options?"

Or: "I notice that my 401(k) isn't growing as fast as I thought it was. Talk to Human Resources about increasing my monthly contributions on Monday. What paperwork do I need?"

Or: "I notice that my Visa could be paid off in three months if I put an extra $200 a month towards that. What can I do to make an extra $200 a month to do that? Dog-walking?"

Step 7.

Take action. Maybe even just one next step. Cancel that gym membership. Call that student loan company. These might not be fun things, but they are worthwhile. KNOW that you are making progress, rather than just worrying.

Step 8.

Plan a reward for getting steps done, even if they are small. For example, make yourself a favorite cup of tea or dance to your favorite song. Do something to recognize the action you just took and celebrate. The acknowledgment will help motivate you to do the next small step... and keep going!

Now that you know know how to use a balance sheet, I'd like to provide you with some things I've learned by working with balance sheets over the years.

The Secret to Financial Security

Financial security does NOT come from receiving a large paycheck. The key to financial security is WHERE that paycheck goes. And the balance sheet is where you can really see where the money is going, long-term. This is the key to establishing true financial security. If you hear of any "secret of the wealthy," this is it: being aware of what your money is *doing*. Be intentional and strategic about where your money goes and where it doesn't.

Directing money into assets creates financial security. Directing money into liabilities creates financial insecurity.

Assets are what give you future freedom. Assets give you options and create opportunities. So you generally want to put your money into assets. Remember, these are things like a savings account, a retirement account, property, or other investments.

Liabilities usually drain your resources and keep you down. This is certainly true for liabilities like credit card debt. But remember, it's not a hard and fast rule for all liabilities. As you learned in the previous chapter, not all debt is bad. In terms of the balance sheet, liabilities can sometimes be used to build assets.

Do you remember how we talked about a mortgage being an example of "good debt" because it helps you to achieve a long-term goal? In terms of the balance sheet, a mortgage (liability) creates the opportunity for you to build an asset (a home). Here's how you can see it happening in real time as you enter your numbers: as you pay off the mortgage, your liabilities go down. As your home increases in value, your assets go up. You watch the scale tip from liability to asset, from negative to positive. That's exactly what you want to see happening in your balance sheet. It helps you to clearly quantify your progress.

"Athletes tend to aim where they look"

Let's go back to debt for a moment. If you are always looking at debt, you will always aim at that and miss the other shots, like a basketball player who's only focused on slam dunks and misses all the jump shots. It's human psychology.

The balance sheet helps you to expand your view. Don't forget your assets! That's where you build wealth. If you include assets in your thinking, then you will tend to aim in that direction. You will move from fearing scarcity to creating abundance. As Earl Nightingale said: "You become what you think about." Be conscious of this and use it to your advantage when you're thinking about your money.

I'm not saying that you should ignore debt—that would be irresponsible. What I am saying is that you should not make debt your sole focus. This is a mistake I see way too many people make, especially in their early years.

When you are focused on building assets, you can "crowd out" your worries about liabilities and the debt, making real progress. "Crowding out" is the idea behind Weight Watchers and other successful diet programs. The idea is this: you can eat as many vegetables as you can imagine! Don't focus on what you *can't* have. That's how unhealthy obsessions are created. Focus instead on what you *can* do. This helps your brain to stay in an abundance mindset ("Wow, look at all these veggies I can eat! There are a ton of them!") instead of dwelling in a scarcity mindset ("I can't have chocolate. I feel deprived. That makes me angry. Feeling angry makes me act out with destructive behaviors. That sets me back even further from my goal.").

Bob Bowman, the trainer of Olympic superstar Michael Phelps, seemed to understand the importance of mindset. He said, "You've got to have the software as well as the hardware to make it work."

For Bob and Michael, the hardware was the physical body. For us, the hardware is the spreadsheet and the dollars. But either way, the software: the mental stamina, the mind game – is just as important as the hardware. To make your money work, you need both the spreadsheet and the mental stamina to stick with it.

The balance sheet builds mental stamina

Good news! Your balance sheet can help you build both stamina and dollars. How? On the mental side, your balance sheet can help you exercise your ability to think long-term. Thinking about your situation while looking at your balance sheet takes you out of the day-to-day that lives in your budget. It helps you to see the longer-term effects of your financial decisions.

On the physical side, updating your balance sheet annually provides you with a container like a time capsule, to show you how far you've come and where you're headed. This is incredibly powerful information! An annual balance sheet offers you a framework in which to set and achieve small goals. Achieving small goals is how the large goals are ultimately reached.

JoAnna said it best:

It's so incredibly REWARDING to go back to your sheet every year. During our annual review, I can see how much I had budgeted for each goal and how much it actually cost, and then I can see what I have achieved. I am always surprised by my progress toward my goals because it doesn't feel that big day to day. But when I type up a summary that says something like: 'I paid off my trip' or 'We finally got new gutters for the house' – it feels like a BIG WIN. Seeing that, I feel that I used my money wisely and I'm enjoying the money I have.

Doing our annual balance sheet allows me to give myself a pat on the back. I'm often surprised by how many financial goals we've accomplished. If we didn't take the time for this recognition each year, I feel that our accomplishments would become invisible, and that's sad.

Our balance sheet also makes me reevaluate my goals. Sometimes I have forgotten I wanted to do something... then at our annual review, I get to ask myself, is it still something I want to do? I can also see what effect one financial decision will have on other financial goals. And that helps me to prioritize. I can choose to skip it or move it up on the scale of priorities. Either way, it helps me feel that I am living life according to what is important to me.

Finally, after I've gotten clarity on what's important, I can look at our entire financial landscape and get creative. If something is important but seems challenging, I can think about: is there another way to do this? It helps my mind to shift from "I can't do this" to "HOW can I do this?"

Balancing Your Assets and Liabilities

So how do you use the balance sheet to help you achieve your Ideal Life vision? In general, the name of the game is to reduce liabilities and build assets.

Sometimes people like to focus on one at a time: assets or liabilities.

For example, maybe one year you decide you want to throw all your additional resources into getting your credit cards paid off. You go all out, cutting back on expenses and living lean. You even decrease or stop the contributions to your retirement account. If that ultimately means you get those credit cards to zero in one year, great! Then you have just given yourself the freedom to redirect next year. You can amp back up on the retirement savings, directing all the money that was going to the credit cards, to your retirement account instead. It's similar to the idea of the Debt Snowball from Chapter Four. Laserlike focus on one thing at a time.

Personally, I find greater satisfaction in doing a little bit of everything. Rather than throwing all of the money I budgeted to improve the balance sheet at one goal, I might put half towards the liabilities and the other half towards the assets. That's my way of thinking—financial multi-tasking.

But there's no wrong answer here as long as you know what you are doing and why. If you are clear on your goal and committed to achieving progress, go for it! Make it work for you.

Your balance sheet will be highly personal and the decisions you make from it will change from year to year. It is a living, breathing document. You can use it as a touchstone that you can come back to any time you are faced with making a difficult financial decision. Even in rough times, your balance sheet can be your ally.

"Money is only a tool. It will take you wherever you wish, but it will not replace you as the driver."

—Ayn Rand

One thing to keep in mind here: Am I telling you to stop spending and having fun, and instead put every penny into savings and assets? No. I believe your quality of life, in the present, is important. What I'm showing you with the balance sheet is how to achieve true balance between your present AND your future.

If you're in your working years, you need to realize that at some point in your life, you won't want to rely on your paycheck for your income anymore. So what can you do? Creating assets gives you the choice to move on, leave that paycheck behind, and live on your own terms. That's because your assets can create the income for you.

How Assets Can Create Income

We will not dive into this right now, but I want to list some of the ways that your assets can create income. Tuck these terms away in your mind for future reference.

- Capital gains

- Dividends

- Interest income

- Rental income

- Real estate income

And the list goes on...

For the moment, just be aware that you build your future financial reality each day during your working years. Your balance sheet can help you remember this when life gets hectic. Use it well. Keep moving from liabilities to assets – and then more assets! – to build your future financial freedom.

Note: Words Matter Just as Much as Numbers Do

You might notice that I have never said anything about a "Net Worth Statement" here. That's intentional. "Net Worth Statement" is often used as a synonym for "Balance Sheet," but I find that the connotations are hugely different and significant.

In my opinion, the tool we've been using in this chapter has nothing to do with your "worth." And I believe the ill-phrased term "net worth" is partly why this tool is often misunderstood. After I started referring to it as a "balance sheet," the tool made more sense to me and my whole experience became more positive.

Going back to Ryan's and my story about how I used to consider working with this tool either self-aggrandizing or deflating, that's when I thought of it in terms of "net worth." It implies judgment. I don't want you to associate this wonderful tool with feeling judged. That isn't what it should be about.

Your experience with your balance sheet should be visionary, not judge-y. It should help you to see the way forward, not smack you down. It should be steadying, like a trusty staff, helping you maintain your balance as you continue your climb up your financial mountains.

"The way to move out of judgment is to move into gratitude."

—*Neale Donald Walsch*

As you step forward each day with your financial choices, you can use your balance sheet as a reminder not only to be patient with yourself and your numbers, but also to be grateful for what you have already accomplished.

The Best Part: Writing It Down

While I was cleaning out my desk recently, I found an old balance sheet with my personal goals from nearly ten years ago. The paper was discolored with age and the handwriting was bad, but the numbers were what struck me more than anything. It was like looking into a time capsule. (Did you ever do one of those as a kid?) I got to see, clearly, a picture of myself and my financial reality ten years ago.

To the present-day me, my past goals appeared modest. But I could recall that at the time they seemed out of my reach. Things like, "buy organic food" (which was expensive) and "go to London" (which was not practical at the time). These things seemed like "pie in the sky" ideas when I had written them. They seemed unattainable. But now, not only were they attainable; I had actually done them.

The moment I found that paper, I felt incredibly blessed. I had not taken the time to stop and realize how far we had come. It was a moment that was both humbling and inspiring.

My wish is that you have these kinds of moments. Writing down your financial goals and dreams will enable you to experience this, years down the road. Doing so creates a precious "time capsule" that you can and should refer to months or years later.

If you have already made it a practice to do this, take the time now to go back and dig out an old spreadsheet or list of goals. Appreciate any evidence of progress that you find and use it as a beacon to light the way to future goals.

The Peaceful Prosperity Mindset: Balance Sheet

I am a whole person—much more than the money in my bank account, my debts, or my assets.

My money life is balanced. I can choose to focus on one goal at a time. I can honor both sides of my balance sheet.

I know where I am going and even if my goals seem far away, I have confidence and faith that I will get there.

I am empowered with the knowledge of where my money is going and confident in my ability to direct it to where it needs to go.

I see things from a higher perspective, knowing that setbacks are temporary, and success is inevitable when I stay focused.

I am flexible with my money goals and flexible with the path to get there. I realize the journey may not look like I envision when I start, but I know I will end up in the right place.

Chapter Six

Money Dates and Money Conversations

The Candy Counter

I stood at the candy counter of a boutique chocolate shop, admiring the treats that sat temptingly behind the cool glass. The delicious smell of chocolate filled the room, making my mouth water. I watched in delight as the chocolatier expertly poured the smooth, rich chocolate into perfect, tiny squares. I was next in line. I was getting ready to purchase these bite-sized luxuries to share with my family over the holidays.

I turned to my brother-in-law who was standing next to me and commented, "You know when I was a kid, my grandmother used to take me to the big department store downtown at Christmas. We would go to the candy counter downstairs—just like this one—and she would let me pick out one treat if I had been good all day while she was shopping."

I turned back to watch the chocolates being poured and reflected, "I always thought that was what it felt like to be rich. Rich people had enough money to spend on delicious treats like this."

"And now here you are," he said simply. "Do you feel rich?"

"Yes," I said, surprising my both brother-in-law and myself.

Tapping Into What Makes YOU Feel Rich

"Feeling rich" is a mindset more than a number. You may not "feel rich" buying chocolate, but I did. "Feeling rich" should be a very personal experience for each of us.

What makes you "feel rich"? There's a meditation in the *Peaceful Prosperity Workbook* you can use if you like. "Feeling rich" is the place to start when setting the stage for a successful money date or money conversation. It's not idle dreaming. Starting with an abundant feeling actually moves you in the direction of making "rich" a reality.

If nothing else, take a few deep breaths to clear your mind and anchor yourself before we move on. Take a quick full-body stretch and let out a sigh. Allow yourself to smile and to feel "rich," "abundant," or "blessed." Then you are ready for your financial work.

How to Take Yourself on a Money Date (Solo)

A money date is just like it sounds: time to shut out the rest of the world and focus on just you and your money for a little while. Think of it as you and your money going out for a date.

If that sounds weird, consider this: your relationship with your finances is like any other human relationship: the more time you devote to it, the more understanding, trust, and positive feelings result. The better you get to know each other, the more the relationship improves. A little time and attention can pay off in big ways.

So let's take some time to think about how we can "date" our money.

"There are three possible parts to a date, of which at least two must be offered: entertainment, food, and affection... Under no circumstances can the food be omitted."

– Judith Martin

"Miss Manners" Judith Martin was on to something here. A key to the money date is to make it fun, satisfying, and emotionally rewarding. Don't chain yourself to your desk and stare at a spreadsheet. (You wouldn't do that on a romantic date, would you?) Set up an environment that makes you feel relaxed, happy, and even eager for what comes next.

Engage All of Your Senses

Before you start a financial task, you need to create an atmosphere so pleasant that you WANT to be there. I like to make it a game to engage all five senses.

In the *Peaceful Prosperity Workbook*, there is a Money Date worksheet to help you get started with this if you need a little inspiration.

For smell, you could light your favorite candle or incense. Sometimes I like to make a cup of tea and let the fragrant beverage transport me to a place of comfort and security.

How about taste? (Here's where Miss Manners' requirement of food comes into play!) I like to have a tasty treat beside me while I work. When I finish one small task, I get to take a bite. Then it's on to the next task and the next bite. To me, it's fun and motivating. How about you? What taste would motivate you on your money date?

Next, what about touch? You could wear a flowy robe or your favorite slippers or the softest sweater you possess. If you like to use pen and paper, what about using a favorite type of paper or a pen that gives you joy as you hold it in your hand?

If you prefer a computer, what about using a colorful mouse or mouse pad that you especially love?

For sound, think about what relaxes you. Is it the sound of ocean waves and seagulls? Raindrops falling on a window? Birdsong in the morning? You can play soothing sounds from any device while you are on your money date. My favorite is to put on some great music. I use different music for different moods: flute music makes me feel peaceful; upbeat rock songs make me feel uplifted; disco makes me want to get up and boogie! Use whatever motivates you for the task at hand.

Finally, sight can be a big motivator, too. Some people like to create a "vision board" with pictures of places or people that are inspiring. Use images and objects that feel expansive to you, to help open your mind to possibilities. If the beach is your favorite place, consider finding a channel on YouTube devoted to beaches, so you can pretend you are on a tropical island. Or perhaps set a beach photo as your background on your computer or phone. Use your imagination!

When you put these pleasant elements together, who wouldn't want to be a part of that, even if the task itself isn't especially fun? I believe that atmosphere is hugely important to get a task done. Think of all the people who do work on laptops at coffee shops: they prefer the coffee shop atmosphere for getting work done. I had a friend tell me she was far more productive in this atmosphere than when she was sitting in an office. Go figure!

Where Should We Go?

Now that you have set the stage, what do you DO on your money date? You may know what you need to do, or you may not have a clue! Don't worry, with practice, this will become more natural (just like dating a human!). Here are a few ideas.

- Pay your household bills

- Pay your credit card

- Enter your numbers into your budget (you can reference the fresh budget sheets you created in the previous chapters!)

- Plan your next large purchase/vacation/self-care

- Work on your tax return information

- File/organize important financial documents

- Look at your savings account/compare rates

- Track your progress toward your goals, including your debt pay-off worksheet

- Look up your credit score

- Update your balance sheet (you have tools for that now!)

- Engage in any of the activities/exercises in this book!

What Do We Do?

Some of these tasks may excite you more than others. That's okay! Here are some ways you can keep the positive vibes going.

"Eat the elephant one bite at a time." Rather than approaching your task as one HUGE thing that MUST get done, break it down into smaller, bite-sized pieces. Your sense of overwhelm will diminish, and your motivation will increase when the task seems simple and doable.

For example, if you are tackling the task of "doing your taxes," rather than telling yourself you will lock yourself into a room and not come out until the task is done, try telling yourself you will simply create a folder for all of this year's tax forms. That's it. Once you've done that, your brain's natural curiosity will probably take over. You may find yourself thinking, "Well now that I've got this folder, I may as well put something into it." Then go ahead. But tell yourself you only need to put one thing in there. Just one form.

Do it, then sit back and give yourself a high five. Feels good, doesn't it? You might begin to feel like an excited child, pleading, "Let's do it again!" Indulge that feeling. Find just one more form and file it. And then one more...

If you get overwhelmed, stop and take a break. Tell yourself you're doing great, and step away from the area for a moment. The moral of this game: You can fool yourself into getting a much larger task done by starting with something small—even if it seems trivial. Lighten the psychological load and you'll likely come out ahead.

Rewards big and small: I believe a key element to achieving goals is rewarding yourself for good behavior, just as you would when training a child or a pet. No matter how old or young we are, we respond to positive reinforcement. Why not use this to your advantage?

For example, I knew a salesperson who would put a chocolate bar on her desk when she had to make phone calls. Each time she completed a call, she would reward herself with a bite of the chocolate bar. This small-step approach helped her to get motivated to make each call, rather than waiting to eat the entire bar only after the entire task was done. Of course, you can celebrate larger tasks with larger rewards, too. For example, let's say you finish gathering all that tax information. That's a big deal! What would help you to recognize and celebrate? A refreshing walk in nature? A luxurious bath? Watching your favorite series on Netflix? Rewards don't have to be expensive or public. Rewards should simply express appreciation and recognition for getting the task done.

When Should We Go Out Again?

With Money Dates, it's important to develop a routine and stick to it. I know this can be the hard part. But if you've created a pleasant atmosphere with the suggestions above, it gets easier. Routines can also help with your time and focus.

For example, I like to do my weekly financial tasks on Saturday mornings. I get on the computer and go through the bank accounts and credit cards, enter my business mileage for the week, and so forth. Doing this weekly takes me less than a half hour. I used to put off these tasks until tax time, when I had to wade through a year's worth of data. Ugh! That was painful. Now I take a few minutes every Saturday morning (not as painful). Then I reward myself with a pancake breakfast with my husband (much more pleasant)!

Whatever your routine is, remember that consistency is key. If you fall off the wagon, so be it. Don't beat yourself up. Get back up and start again.

So often we take ourselves too seriously when it comes to our finances. Yes, finances are important—don't get me wrong—but even important things in life can be improved by approaching them with a sense of humor and playfulness.

Having playful money dates can help take the fear out of finance. And you might even find that you get more done!

Money Dates With a Partner

"Alone, we can do so little... Together, we can do so much..."

– Helen Keller

Couples have a unique opportunity to build a bright, positive future together with the power of TWO. But it's not always smooth sailing. Even the happiest couples often bump into difficulties when discussing money. And it's no wonder!

Personal finance is a very private topic. For many people, it's a topic even more private than sex. (Think about it... You may talk about your sex life with your closest friend, but when's the last time you talked to them about your household income?) Because it is so private, it is also an infrequent topic, so we don't get a chance to practice talking about this, either. So how DO you have comfortable and productive money conversations?

Here's a hint: Did you know that we all have a preferred style of communicating when we are talking about money?

Finance-related discussions are more productive and less volatile when we understand our communication style and that of our spouse/partner.

In the *Peaceful Prosperity Workbook*, there is an exercise called "Communication Preferences," which was created by Susan Bradley, founder of the Sudden Money Institute. The exercise is designed to help you quickly identify your primary preferences when talking about money. With couples, the key is to have each person do the exercise on their own first. Then you can come together and explore the answers. I have seen this single exercise (and the ensuing conversation) profoundly change couples' lives!

The Newlyweds

Justin and Bianca were in the final planning stages of their wedding. They were tallying RSVPs and counting down the days until the big event. They came in to see me because they wanted to get started off on the right foot in their marriage, and they knew that money was an especially important topic for newlyweds.

When they came in, they were visibly nervous. Bianca's shoulders were hunched and Justin's jaw was tight. I asked them to complete the Communication Preferences exercise separately. I could feel the concentration as they each did so. What followed was an enlightening conversation.

One of Justin's strong preferences was, "Allow me time to process my response." He explained that when he was thinking about money, he was weighing all the different options in his head. That analysis took all his mental bandwidth. He didn't have enough left to verbalize his thoughts while they were being formed. After he had time to sort everything out in his mind, then he would willingly be ready to share his questions and conclusions.

Bianca's face changed as she listened to this. "I never knew that," she said quietly. "I always thought you just didn't want to share your thoughts with me." The loving look that passed between them was a beautiful thing.

In her preferences, Bianca included, "Look for ways to minimize the risks." Taking any action that she felt would expose them to danger or harm made her extremely uncomfortable. Before making decisions, she wanted to understand exactly what the risks were, and then exactly how to mitigate those risks. Once she had this information, Bianca said she would feel more confident about taking action. "Of course!" said Justin. "That's easy! I always thought you just didn't trust me and didn't want to do anything."

"No way!" Bianca laughed. "You've made good decisions in the past. I just need to hear your thoughts on what we do in the future."

When they left, they were laughing and holding hands. I'm pretty confident that they are building a bright future for themselves right now.

Having productive money conversations is a skill. It doesn't happen overnight. Keep in mind that it can take years to build trust and focus. Give-and-take is a natural part of the process. Below are some ideas on how to work through this together.

Understand and Support Where the Other Person is Coming From

> *"Seek first to understand, then to be understood."*
>
> *— Steven Covey*

This means doing a lot of listening, rather than judging. Realize that you and your spouse will probably never look at money the same way—and this is a good thing! Different perspectives can help to make you both stronger in the long run.

Think about how you can learn from each other. If you are making decisions together, how can you see the money issue from a "we" perspective, rather than a "you" and "I" perspective? If you can focus on working towards common goals, rather than pulling in opposite directions, you'll get farther.

Mary shared this creative solution: when she and her husband approached a money conversation, they dressed in their favorite sports team jerseys. This helped them to remember they were "on the same team." Starting with common ground helps you both to get a sure footing before climbing to the harder stuff.

When a financial decision comes up, what can you agree upon? How can you come to a compromise? Or perhaps you can agree to work on one goal for a while, then work on a different goal, so that you are addressing both eventually.

Recognize the Emotional Aspect of Any Money Conversation for Both of You

Anyone who thinks money is purely a logical game of mathematics is fooling themselves. (You know this by now!) Money comes with multiple emotional layers, often created by years of baggage: family history and influence (positive or negative), childhood stories (good or bad), past experiences (observed or lived), decisions made, and their outcomes (wonderful or awful). All this money baggage and even money shame are very real and visceral. The stories we carry can be uncomfortable. But they are not "wrong" or even necessarily "bad." Acknowledging money emotions can be empowering if explored lovingly and without judgment.

If you are willing to explore your money story with your partner and encourage them to do the same, the experience can make you both stronger and closer in all aspects of your lives.

Side note: not all money conversations have to *start* with your partner. Perhaps there are some money topics you want to explore on your own before you discuss them together. As one woman observed: "I want to deal with my own stuff before I can help him deal with his." That's fine. You can go back to the first part of this chapter and make a money date with yourself first, so you can feel on solid ground when you bring up a potentially sensitive topic with another person.

Watch the Jargon!

If both of you are comfortable with financial terms and concepts, great! Often, however, that is not the case. I find that usually, one person is more comfortable with financial language, and the other is not. That's okay, but you need to have some sort of common language so you can communicate with each other. Only then can you set goals and agree upon the steps toward your goals.

Too often the person who is comfortable with financial terms leads the way, and the person who is uncomfortable buries their head in the sand. As a friend of mine says, this is "sub-optimal." And it isn't how a successful team runs the race.

Think of this like running a money marathon relay.

If you're the one comfortable with money language, you've got the baton and you're running. If you run the entire race without passing the baton, you're not running a relay, you're just running. That can get exhausting. And that's not much fun for your partner. You need to remember your partner is running alongside you. Anticipate your partner coming along to grab the baton. You need to give it to them with the assurance that they will finish their part of the race successfully. Remember, each of you has strengths that can help the team go farther than you can alone. So look back and notice: are you remembering to hand off your baton? Or have you left your partner in the dust?

"In teamwork, silence isn't golden. It's deadly."

— Mark Sanborn

If you're the partner uncomfortable with money talk, remember that you have a voice! Speak up. Ask questions and keep asking until you are comfortable with what is going on. Try to silence any negative voices that pop up in your head and tell you that "you should know this already." Go back to Chapter One and remind yourself how to silence those "foul voices on the air." Remember that you are important and your partner needs your help.

When running a relay, you both have to know how to hold the baton, how to pass it off, and how to communicate with your teammate. Running a relay is an exercise in communication, timing, and training. You must have a plan as a TEAM, not as two individual runners, to win the marathon.

What if the conversation stalls?

Don't give up! Here are some things you can try:

Build on past "wins." Stop and reflect on something you've accomplished together to remind and reinforce your positive feelings of being a team. For example, before launching into a full financial review, share a happy memory of a time when you worked together on something. It could be planning a trip or fixing the dishwasher. Have fun with it!

Try an old improv technique called "Yes, and..." In improv, you've got to keep the skit going no matter what. So rather than saying "No, but..." which can kill the conversation, actors are taught to use the phrase "Yes, and..." to keep moving forward. This can be a helpful tool in a money conversation.

For example: "I'm afraid we're overspending."

"Yes, and I think that may be because we eat out a lot."

"Yes, and I'd love to eat at home more often to improve my cooking skills."

"Yes, and that could help us save on gas since we won't be driving around town as much."

"Yes, and I hate getting dressed up and going out, anyway. Let's have dinner in our PJs!"

The "Yes, and" game keeps the line of communication open because it challenges your brain to build on the previous thought rather than negate it and insert your own. It's a valuable life skill! It can also encourage creativity and foster brainstorming—great tools to use when tackling difficult issues together.

<u>"Thank you for sharing."</u> If "Yes, and..." becomes a little too difficult, you can always go back to an old standby: "Thank you for sharing." Then follow up with an open-ended question.

For example: "I'm afraid we're overspending."

"Thank you for sharing that. What makes you think so?"

The first statement acts as a validation to help establish that this is a safe place to share opinions. The second part, the question, encourages the conversation to continue.

I hope these techniques help you to approach the topic of money with someone. You can use these tips in any money conversation, not just with a spouse. You can try them with a child or a parent, as well.

In my experience, the key to working together successfully is to recognize this truth: money is messy. If you are willing to share your past money stories without judgment, you can create a new money story together. You also might consider going back to Chapter One and talking about the "Digging Down to the Roots" exercise together. What money stories do you have in common from your past? What stories do you want to change together? What stories will you create in your future?

Changing the Past

Every quarter, Anthony insisted that he and his wife Ella have regular money conversations. He wanted to go over their account statements. It was important to him that Ella knew where they stood and what was going on. Ella put up with these meetings because she dearly loved Anthony and wanted him to be happy. But she never exactly relished them or understood why they were so important to her husband.

Then one day they began talking about their childhood memories, and Ella heard a story she had not heard before. Anthony had watched his parents go through an ugly divorce when he was relatively young. Ella knew this. What she didn't know was the level of detail Anthony had noticed, even as a child, and how it had affected him. He had observed his parents using money as a tool to punish each other for emotional infidelities. They manipulated money to control the people around them and to get others "on their side" during the divorce. Both parents hid money from each other; they used that as an additional reason to distrust each other and proclaim that the other was a bad person.

"I made a vow to NEVER be like that when I got married," Anthony said gravely.

"That's why you insist on these quarterly money discussions?" Ella asked.

"Of course," he said, concerned. "I never want us to hide things from each other like that. I always want you to know exactly where we stand." He paused. "I guess that's an important way I want to say I love you," he concluded.

Ella was touched. She had never thought of their quarterly discussions as an expression of love before. As you can imagine, their money conversations were far sweeter for both of them after that realization.

Considerations When Combining Finances

"Should we combine our finances?" is a common question I hear. Most people seem to think there is a "right" way and a "wrong" way to answer this when entering a marriage or long-term partnership.

I'm sorry to disappoint you if you think that's true. There are no hard and fast rules about combining finances, and no "right" or "wrong" answer (which surprises some people). It doesn't matter your age, gender, sex, or tax bracket. Instead, it's a matter of personal preference and your dynamic as a couple.

It's important to note that I have seen couples achieve their goals and have wonderful, healthy relationships using many different methods. The method you choose isn't the most important thing. The most important thing is the commitment and communication of both partners. (Hmm, kinda sounds like marriage itself, doesn't it?)

Method One: One Joint Account: All sources of income go into one place (a joint bank account), and all expenses come out from that one place.

Works best for: couples with one income source (i.e., one is the breadwinner, the other is the stay-at-home parent) or with couples where one partner is comfortable with budgeting and finance, while the other is terrified of it. There's nothing wrong with this. Learning to play to your strengths is an important part of any marriage or partnership.

Pros: complete transparency. Both partners can see what goes in and out, down to the penny. Some couples say this creates trust.

Cons: other couples say this creates an atmosphere of judgment and resentment because seeing where every penny goes causes fights over what money "should" be spent on. If that's the case for you, consider the next option:

Method Two: Yours, Mine, and Ours Accounts: Each partner has their own accounts (yours/mine), and then there is also one joint account (ours) for shared finances.

This requires a conversation to set up, which is a good thing. For this method, couples need to agree upon what expenses are to be "shared" (i.e., the house payment, utilities, grocery store runs, eating out) and what is not shared (i.e., clothing, haircuts, hobbies, personal gifts). They also need to agree on how much each person contributes to the joint account each month. For example, 50% of each person's paycheck? Or a set dollar amount? Does one person make significantly more money than the other, and does this mean that person puts in more? Again, there's no right or wrong answer here. Whatever answer you come up with needs to make sense and feel fair to both.

<u>Works best for</u>: couples where both partners are relatively comfortable with managing money; or couples with some reason in their personal history (e.g. divorce) that makes separate accounts feel more comfortable.

<u>Pros</u>: some couples say this type of working together is preferable because it helps keep them focused on the "big picture" items in their financial life, rather than fighting over smaller financial items. It can also help each partner maintain a sense of autonomy and control while establishing a sense of fairness in the shared account.

<u>Cons</u>: some couples say this makes them feel too separated. Based on your past experiences with money, and your personal money beliefs, this method could feel "weird" to you. If so, you could opt for Method One.

The Big Picture

The goal when combining finances is not for either of you to be perfect with your money. Rather, it is to come up with a system that works for both of you—one that feels fair and honest, and one that each partner can willingly commit to. The way to achieve this is through communication.

A financial planning colleague, Hannah Moore, CFP®, commented, "Communicating about money... should be a top priority in your relationship. Not communicating is also one of the biggest mistakes newlyweds make with their finances." I think she is so right!

Talking about money with your honey may not be the most romantic thing that you do, but it may be one of the most important, and ultimately rewarding, things that you do together as a couple.

OK, we're talking, but I still think we can do better...

Have you considered seeking a neutral third party, such as a financial planner? Often the most useful thing I do in a couples meeting is to facilitate the money discussion. Both spouses have different takes on their money situation, and usually, both are right about certain aspects. But it can be challenging to see the other person's point of view. That's where having a neutral third party can help.

Someone like a financial planner can help couples interpret each other's perspectives, validate viewpoints, and gently redirect where needed. A good planner can point out the strengths that each partner already has, and then show the couple how to use these strengths to build something really special together.

"Coming together is a beginning. Keeping together is progress. Working together is success."

— Henry Ford

Money conversations are not easy! But they can be a truly special opportunity to learn about each other, to talk about goals and dreams, and to work together as a couple.

Remember that this process takes time and continual effort. Like growing a garden, you can't simply throw out a few seeds and expect a paradise to spring out of the ground. You've got to give it care and attention, tending to it lovingly, consistently. It is only over time that things take root and flourish.

My husband and I didn't always see eye-to-eye at first, as I mentioned in the Balance Sheet chapter. But we kept working together, taking breaks, making compromises, and keeping the lines of communication open. Now it feels very different from when we first started. We have so much FUN as we tend our financial garden! Appreciating each other and communicating are the keys to getting to this stage in a relationship. You now have some tools to do this! I hope they help you as they have helped us.

The Peaceful Prosperity Mindset: Money Dates

I create a supportive, pleasant environment before I begin financial tasks. I celebrate my accomplishments, even if they seem small.

I handle money conversations with compassion for myself and others. I am courageously honest.

I am aware of and listen to the language I use when speaking about money. I encourage supportive words and phrases when talking to myself and others.

My voice is important and my opinions about money are valid and valuable. I honor my opinions and those of my partner.

I know each person has their own money stories and money baggage. I give myself permission to be different from my partner yet confident we can work together on our goals.

My partner and I are on the same team. Together we can get farther ahead than either of us could do alone. I look for strengths within each of us and nurture those strengths to support our money goals.

CONGRATULATIONS ON COMPLETING THE SUMMIT: EXPANDING YOUR VISION

Are you seeing things a bit differently now? You should be in a very different place from where you started.

Take a moment to reflect on the hard work you've done so far—from mindset to budget to balance sheet. You're climbing up the mountain of finance! Did you believe you could do it?

What's the trek been like so far? There's a page in the *Peaceful Prosperity Workbook* to jot down your thoughts if you like.

You've now built your foundation. Where else do you want to go?

Rest now and drink in the beautiful vistas you have seen so far. Tomorrow, you can decide on the next trail you'll take. This is just the beginning.

Conclusion

Now You Can (But You Always Could)

M y Wish For You

I want you to experience peaceful prosperity. You are the reason I wrote this book.

My wish is not for you to be a perfect budgeter or to have the perfect retirement plan. My wish is for you to realize your skills and your potential. My wish is for you to realize that <u>you can,</u> no matter where you are right now in life.

You <u>can</u> use money as a wonderful tool in your life to express joy, love, and authentic caring.

You <u>can</u> change the story you've learned about money and how it operates in your life.

You <u>can</u> use your creativity to manage your expenses and earn more than you think.

You <u>can</u> make sense of your debt and move beyond it.

You <u>can</u> build a vision of the future you want, and you <u>can</u> find the opportunities in your balance sheet that will get you there.

You <u>can</u> enjoy the experience of working with your money and make more progress when you are relaxed.

You <u>can</u> have productive, fun, meaningful conversations about money with others in your life.

"You're braver than you believe, stronger than you seem, and smarter than you think."

—Winnie the Pooh

I hope you believe this by now.

I hope you hear me and all the women who have traveled before you, cheering you on as you climb.

Let's keep on climbing together.

References and Recommended Reading

There are LOTS of good financial books out there!

The following are either referenced in this book or have influenced my thinking about finance in some significant way. Enjoy!

Smart Women Finish Rich by David Bach

www.davidbach.com

The Ten Commandments of Financial Happiness by Jean Chatzky

www.jeanchatzky.com

Mindset by Carol Dweck

A Year of Mindful Wellness by Lisa Feder

www.beingwellyoga.com

F.I.R.E. movement and *Your Money or Your Life*

www.yourmoneyoryourlife.com

The Big Leap by Gay Hendricks

www.hendricks.com

The Psychology of Money by Morgan Housel

www.morganhousel.com

Rich Dad, Poor Dad by Robert Kiyosaki

www.richdad.com

Sudden Money by Mary Martin and Susan Bradley

www.suddenmoney.com

Financial Recovery by Karen McCall

www.moneygrit.com

Hannah Moore, CFP® / www.guidingwealth.com

Total Money Makeover by Dave Ramsey

www.ramseysolutions.com

I Will Teach You to be Rich by Remit Sethi

www.iwillteachyoutoberich.com

Simon Sinek / www.simonsinek.com

The Millionaire Next Door by Thomas J. Stanley and William D. Danko

www.themillionairenextdoor.com

Overcoming Underearning by Barbara Stanny

www.barbara-huson.com

The Art of Money by Bari Tessler

www.baritessler.com

My Own Two Feet: A Modern Girl's Guide to Personal Finance by Manisha Thakor and Sharon Kedar

Bonus Material

Would you like to continue taking the fear out of finance?

Visit the Peaceful Prosperity website for more!

peaceful-prosperity.com

WORKSHOPS and ONE-ON-ONE COACHING

Engage with other money adventurers in an intimate, small group setting, or engage with me one-on-one. We discuss the concepts in the book and explore your own personal money story. I answer your questions and help you find solutions to your financial challenges. Visit the website for availability and dates: peaceful-prosperity.com.

BOOK TWO: *Creating Your Financial Future*

The next book in the *Peaceful Prosperity* series is *Creating Your Financial Future*. In this book, you will learn the terminology and concepts, the "nuts and bolts," that will empower you even more by:

... demystifying investments,

... investigating insurance with intention,

... exploring how to create beautiful bridges for those who follow after you,

... reimagining retirement.

NEWSLETTER

Sign up at peaceful-prosperity.com to receive monthly tips, affirmations, and fresh ideas. Subscribers also get updates on new releases and access to new offerings before they are available to the public.

YOUTUBE

Go to peaceful-prosperity.com and click on "Resources" to access free videos I post periodically, full of encouragement and insights.

About the Author

Laura Redfern, CFP®, CeFT® is a financial planner, writer, coach, and creator of the Peaceful Prosperity Workshops, a series of financial education classes for women.

Laura never thought her career path would be in finance. With a background in Theatre Arts and British Literature, she always assumed she'd end up teaching, helping students to discover the power of language. But when she moved to Texas in 2002 and began working for an insurance company, she discovered the power of an entirely different language: the language of finance.

Laura earned her Certified Financial Planner™ designation in 2011, after working for nearly ten years in the financial services industry. In addition to investment management and retirement planning, Laura helped clients navigate life's difficult transitions (divorce, inheritance, and retirement, to name a few). This experience fueled her interest in the Certified Financial Transitionist® designation, which she earned in 2020. She now advises clients on both sides of money: the technical and the deeply personal.

An active member of Toastmasters International, Laura has earned the Distinguished Toastmaster designation (the highest educational level in Toastmasters), as well as having served as Club President, Club Coach, and Division Director.

Laura currently resides in Austin, Texas with her husband, Ryan. When she's not writing, you can find her drinking tea, eating tacos, doing yoga, or binge-watching Disney movies.

For more information or to contact Laura, please visit:

peaceful-prosperity.com

Made in the USA
Las Vegas, NV
19 August 2023

76318633R00115